CRISIS MINISTRY: A HANDBOOK

Crisis

A HANDBOOK

Ministry

daniel bagby

SMYTH&HELWYS
PUBLISHING, INCORPORATED   MACON, GEORGIA

Smyth & Helwys Publishing, Inc.
6316 Peake Road
Macon, Georgia 31210-3960
1-800-747-3016
©2002 by Smyth & Helwys Publishing
All rights reserved.
Printed in the United States of America.

The paper used in this publication meets the min-
imum requirements of American National
Standard for Information Sciences—Permanence
of Paper for Printed Library Materials.
ANSI Z39.48–1984. (alk. paper)

Library of Congress Cataloging-in-Publication Data

Bagby, Daniel G.
    Crisis Ministry: A Handbook/
    by Daniel G. Bagby.
    p.   cm.
    ISBN 978-1-57312-370-9 (alk. paper)
    1. Church work—Handbooks, manuals, etc.
    I. Title.

    BV4400 .B27 2002
    253'.7—dc21

                                        2002009680
                                            CIP

Table of Contents

Introduction

Every human being deals with changes and transitions that create anxieties and challenge our capacity to cope. Ministers and other caregivers are expected to help people in crises, especially those who belong to the "household of faith" (Galatians 6:10). This guide was designed as a resource for religious caregivers who are asked to give immediate assistance to individuals and families in crises. As a pastor I have shared the ministry of caregiving with deacons in three different congregations during a span of twenty-four years. As a teacher in the seminary, I've had the privilege of working with many deacon groups and other caregiving teams in local congregations. The sacred trust bestowed by congregations on clergy and laypeople alike determines that both are regularly invited to minister in the most significant life challenges. Some of these critical events are positive and celebrative, and some of them are traumatic and distressing to parishioners.

Ministers struggle to respond effectively to the more difficult and destructive crises human beings face. Deacons and other caregivers wrestle with the delicate task of providing a redemptive response to parishioners facing challenging circumstances. For a variety of reasons (trust, availability, flexibility, mobility) parishioners (and perhaps even the general population) apparently still turn first to church communities for help during a crisis (David K. Switzer, *The Minister as Crisis Counselor* [Nashville: Abingdon Press, 1974] 21).

Caregivers in the church share a common characteristic: almost all of them feel unprepared and inadequate to offer such help. What can be done to help these "frontline" respondents who receive emergency invitations from hurting people experiencing deepest distress? What can we do to better equip our clergy and lay caregivers in the art of "spiritual first aid" and provide them with tools to render initial care to traumatized parishioners facing difficult situations?

The following pages are an attempt to provide help for ministers—and other caregivers—who must respond to individuals and families seeking help during the initial stages of particular crises. The hope is not to equip caregivers to provide extensive or complete assistance for people under pressure, but to guide them to know how to help in the first moments of a difficult event: what to say, what to do, who to call, to whom to refer them, and to what resources to direct them in a time of specific need.

The subjects and issues mentioned in these pages are those I and other caregivers have encountered most often as crises in the lives of parishioners during the course of ministry. The comments that follow are abbreviated because people facing emergencies have little time to read. This guide of first steps assumes that the reader is a caregiver in a local church and that a faith system directs the process of rendering "first care." Resources for appropriate referral are mentioned at the end of each topic, and further reading is suggested for more extensive care. In each case we assume that the emergency caregiver is not an expert in the issue, but one who can direct hurting people to proper sources of care, coping, and help.

Initial pages explain why we care in the church. The final section of this care guide focuses on specific helps in general caregiving and guidelines for those who care for people during celebrative crises in their lives, since these occasions can also evoke anxiety, energy, and stress. The information listed under each title assumes that redemptive caregiving is the primary goal in each intervention, regardless of how the crisis began.

Why We Care

We care because God cared for us first in making us, in sharing creation with us, and in inviting us to an ongoing relationship of purpose. God has coached and prompted us through Scripture, patriarch, king, prophet, priest, and apostle—but most clearly through Jesus Christ, our complete model of care (John 1:9-17).

We care because God has shown all who follow that being in God's image means remaining faithful in relationships regardless of what has happened. God regularly disagreed with Israel about her priorities and behavior, but never abandoned her because of her actions. Fidelity in a relationship has little to do with another person's behavior; it is a question of how God loves—continually (Romans 8:38-39). God has always offered a visible presence for the people of God in every crisis, and asks us to do the same. The cloud by day, the pillar of fire by night, the prophet, the ark of the covenant, the king, the tent of meeting, the incarnation of Jesus Christ, and the church (the body of Christ!) are reminders that God has always given followers a tangible presence in their need. We are called to be God's visible presence in people's lives.

Following the example of the prophet Isaiah, and of Jesus Christ as he opened his ministry, we are called as God's people to help "release the captives" and "to bring good tidings to the afflicted" (Isaiah 61:1-4). Following Christ's model, the people of God are also called to "proclaim good news to the poor, to announce release to the captives, and the recovery of sight to the blind, and to set at liberty those who are oppressed, to proclaim the acceptable year of the Lord" (Luke 4:18-19). God's people need to be released from their burdens and struggles. Because God has taken risks with us by loving us and giving us freedom, and came to us in the vulnerable form of Jesus Christ to show us how to live and love, we too are to risk in love for there is no way to love from a distance. Being in the image of love (God), we are to risk as God does—coming into our chaotic world as a fragile infant in order to deliver love personally (John 1:14).

God sought and loved a forgotten and neglected people (Israel), and Christ regularly took initiative to offer care and grace to the ignored and wounded of his day (Luke 19:2). We too, are called as the "Body of Christ" to love as he loved, and seek out the wounded and the devalued members of society (Matthew 5:3-11). Jesus Christ called any who would follow him to become servants as he was, and to wash feet and redeem lives (John 13:12-17). Christ showed us that serving our brothers and sisters is God's way of expressing the highest form of care. Because God loved us enough to place us in families, and because Christ called his followers to act as a family of compassion, we represent a community of brothers and sisters related to each other by a sacred bond (John 19:26-27). Because Christ gave us a new identity, we no longer work only for ourselves, but work with the comforting presence of God's Spirit, so that none of God's children are abandoned, or left "desolate" (John 14:15-18; 15:12-17). As Christ came not to condemn but to redeem, we are charged to seek redemptive ways to heal broken spirits (John 3:17).

Abortion

When an Abortion Has Occurred

1) The decision to undergo an abortion is one of the most difficult decisions a woman makes. Unlike the spontaneous loss of a fetus (see **Death and Dying** and **Grief**), being involved in the decision to terminate a pregnancy can create agonizing emotional and spiritual turmoil.

2) The removal of a fetus by human intervention prior to its attaining capacity for living independent of the mother is usually called an abortion. Such a procedure may be undertaken for several different reasons—to save the life of a mother, to discontinue a pregnancy caused by rape, to interrupt a pregnancy when the fetus appears to have severe brain damage, and other reasons. Don't assume you know why the decision was made.

3) When a family member reports that such a procedure has taken place, caregivers should first analyze their own feelings about abortion. Strong feelings or prejudgments can interfere with their capacity to offer help or support to a person recovering from an abortion. Remember that doctors are required to render aid to wounded persons regardless of the circumstances under which they were hurt. If your beliefs about this issue are so strong that you cannot help a parishioner, you must be honest about your limitation. Offer to call someone else the person trusts. People who have undergone an abortion do not need additional stress, grief, or guilt placed upon them as they struggle to put their lives back together.

4) The next question concerns the physical safety of the patient. Was the surgery uneventful (no physical problems)? Is the patient still in the hospital? At home? Any complications? Do they need help getting home?

5) The next question, concerning confidentiality and privacy, precedes initial steps in mobilizing community resources. Who knows about the procedure, and should it be shared with anyone else at this time? If the church community is to be used as a resource for care, it is wise to "rehearse" with the patient how much is to be shared—and with whom. Consider whether the event should be interpreted simply as "a surgical procedure" to the church community, for the sake of privacy and care.

6) Remember that an abortion is indeed a surgical intervention and should be treated as such. Medical advice on taking days away from school or work, physical recovery, and limited activity are to be taken seriously.

7) Does the person (or the family) need practical support right now? Suggestions are providing meals, offering care at home, securing medical attention of some kind, doing the laundry, helping with transportation, and making phone calls.

8) If the pastor did not receive the news, ask the family's permission to inform the pastor so that he or she may offer initial pastoral care. People who undergo an abortion experience the event as a loss, even if the pregnancy was not desired. Grief loss produces a series of reactions that include numbness, depression, flow of emotion, anger, guilt, sudden and stabbing memories, and severe mood swings (see **Grief**).

9) Ask the person (or the family) if there is a small group of supportive friends with whom the patient can share her many feelings. Experience has shown that people who undergo pregnancy loss find it helpful to talk about their feelings with someone who will neither

judge them nor offer unwanted advice. They need someone who will mainly provide them the service of listening (see **Listening**), a healing gift of active presence as they process the experience by talking through it.

10) Remember that various family members may have different responses to the loss of a pregnancy. Your contribution may be to make sure that every family member's feelings are heard   and acknowledged.

11) If family members experience tension because of strong disagreement about the surgery, you may suggest that they seek help with a counselor or pastor who can help them sort out different feelings and avoid unnecessary pain and misunderstanding. Individuals or families who feel awkward discussing this issue with their pastor could see a pastoral counselor (available in most communities), or a counselor in private practice who will honor their privacy and respect their different responses.

12) Remember that listening to people's feelings is one of your best contributions at this point—not arguing with their feelings. Survivors of abortion usually need three qualities in a first conversation:

• trust in the person with whom they share;
• acknowledgment of the reality of the procedure;
• an opportunity to process their feelings about the experience.

13) Abortion carries quite a stigma in the religious world. Many people struggle with whether having an abortion is taking a life. You should probably avoid theological arguments and let a pastor or trusted friend share more about this question at another time. Ask yourself: How do I most serve a redemptive purpose in this person's life right now?

14) If the idea of a support group sounds helpful to the parishioner, several organizations may provide extended care and counseling. The

local Crisis Pregnancy Center usually offers alternatives to abortion. It also offers particular support for survivors of spontaneous (non-induced) abortions, and for pregnant women who wish to continue their pregnancy and offer the baby for adoption. Planned Parenthood offers support to women following an induced abortion (chosen), and can often provide group support following the surgery.

15) Survivors of an abortion often feel that they have no right to grieve a loss they chose to undergo. Help them realize that they have the right to grieve, and that there are people who can help them walk through their bereavement. In the long run, survivors of abortion will profit most from a confidential grief support group, and from particular caregivers who understand the loss. Ask your pastor or a mental health worker in your area for help in locating these groups.

16) The man involved in the pregnancy should not be ignored in the process of caring for the woman. The delicate and difficult issue of including the potential father and his feelings is one best left with pastors and mental health professionals, since there are so many aspects to consider.

For further reading:

Johann Christoph Arnold, *Why Forgive?* (Farmington PA: The Plough Publishing House, 2000).

Michael Jacobs, ed., *The Care Guide* (London: Cassell, 1995).

Dena Rosenbloom & Mary Beth Williams, *Life After Trauma* (New York: Guilford Publications, 2000).

Granger Westberg, *Good Grief: A Constructive Approach to the Problem of Loss* (Minneapolis: Fortress Press, 1986).

When an Abortion Has Not Yet Occurred

1) If you are asked to help before a decision on abortion has been made, listen carefully to the person's feelings and the feelings family or friends may have. Also check your own feelings. Your opinion, if strong, will surface and affect how you express your care.

2) If you sense that your emotions about the subject are so strong that you cannot help a pregnant woman evaluate her options, suggest that she share her feelings with another caregiver. Also suggest that she (and her family, if applicable) talk with the pastor about the decision.

3) Those who choose to continue the pregnancy to full term need medical care and can be helped by several groups: Crisis Pregnancy Centers (usually staffed by people who believe in carrying a pregnancy to birth), Planned Parenthood, and local medical clinics. People who choose to discontinue the pregnancy can be assisted by Planned Parenthood clinics and private medical groups.

4) Remember that a decision to maintain or discontinue a pregnancy involves intense emotions (both for the patient and her family), and that many different feelings will surface, including contradictory emotions and responses. Pray for the people involved, and be patient with them as they struggle with anger, guilt, relief, and shame that can surface and resurface several times. Make sure they receive continued pastoral and medical care in the months following these decisions.

5) The process of recovery from the emotional and physical impact of an abortion continues for a long time. Anniversaries and new pregnancies can also trigger heavy memories. Remember parishioners who have trusted you with this significant time in their lives. Pray for individuals and families regardless of their decisions, for they are children of God.

Abuse

There are four identified kinds of abuse: Emotional, Physical, Sexual, and Spiritual.

Emotional Abuse

1) Until recently, few people recognized emotional abuse, because for years yelling, screaming, and belittling people has been such a common practice in families. Today, however, more people are aware of the destructive and demeaning power of emotional abuse. If a parishioner has come to you because they are being verbally oppressed, the first care you can offer them is to validate their feelings as legitimate.

2) Caring for those who have been emotionally abused involves understanding the humiliating power of verbal attacks. Children are regularly controlled with abusive language that shames them into believing they are not valued by their parents. Young children who are regularly subjected to such verbal lashings often grow up believing that God also holds them in low account, since their parents attack the child's sense of self-worth in trying to provide discipline.

3) Emotionally abused people need to be heard and believed. They also need to be affirmed as lovable and valued. Children subjected to a regular dose of demeaning messages grow up with a low sense of self-worth. Personal interest and care shown by an adult they trust can be of great encouragement to them.

4) Sometimes children—and even spouses—are not in a position to leave an abusive relationship. If you have a trusted relationship with an abusive parent, you may be able to approach the problem by pointing out that they seem frustrated and stressed with their many obligations, and that they may want to look into ways of coping with their stress so that they can maintain emotional control under pressure.

5) Most abusive parents are stressed people with poor techniques for coping with frustration. Emotionally abusive people usually express their frustration and stress in explosive outbursts against family members with whom it is "safe" to lose control. They rarely understand how destructive and overpowering their verbal attacks are.

6) A child's instinctive wince at a gesture or movement that appears harmful can be a sign of physical or emotional abuse. Other signs of abuse are swollen or discolored faces, facial signs of pain at the slightest touch, a careless act of cruelty to a pet, fear of being left alone with a particular parent, and an unusual tendency to remain withdrawn around adults. However, abuse can be disguised or hidden, and no signs may be apparent at all. Take a child seriously when they courageously mention any unusually aggressive behavior of an adult.

7) If you suspect a family member or family of being abusive, take any opportunity to invite them to support and training sessions that assist parents with discipline and frustration management. Better still, encourage your congregation to offer Parent Discipline Classes for young parents. Many parents discipline their children when they are intensely angry with them, and thus overreact to certain issues and become abusive. Parent Effectiveness Training (PET) is an excellent teaching program and book that can be taught in sessions at church as a prevention to harsh and ineffective methods of parental punishment. Henry Cloud and John Townsend's book *Boundaries for Kids* is another excellent resource for church discussions on discipline with parents.

For further reading:

Dan Harrison, *Strongest in the Broken Places* (Downer's Grove IL: InterVarsity Press, 1990).

Marti Tamm Loring, *Emotional Abuse* (New York: Lexington Books, 1994).

Cynthia Monahon, *Children and Trauma* (San Francisco: Jossey-Bass Publishers, 1993).

Lewis B. Smedes, *Shame and Grace: Healing the Shame We Don't Deserve* (San Francisco: HarperSanfrancisco, 1993).

Physical Abuse

1) One in four families in the United States experiences abuse, and often church families manage this problem secretly in their homes. Victims are often threatened physically if they betray the family secret, and they are held responsible for embarrassing the family or "starting trouble."

2) Family members often protect abusive relatives and have an unwritten agreement not to expose the abuser.

3) Victims of abuse may call you in urgent need to find a safe place to go until an abusive family member has calmed or left the house. Most cities have family abuse shelters, and your church should have that phone number available (Abuse Shelters never give out addresses). Children can often be accommodated along with their parent. Look for help under the following organizations: Family Abuse Shelter, Family Shelter, The Salvation Army, and any other charity organizations communities provide. If no shelter is immediately at hand, a police station may be the quickest aid.

4) Victims of physical abuse fear for their safety and especially the safety of their children. Most spouses refuse to report abusers for fear of retaliation on their children, themselves, or their property.

5) You should know that abusers don't stop after one violent incident. Abusers have usually learned poor coping skills for stress, and they often learned abusive behavior from their own parents. Abusers need

help in setting controls over their behavior and in learning better ways to cope with frustration.

6) When a victim calls, make sure she (usually a female, but not always) is in a safe place at that moment, or can get out of harm's way quickly. If children are present, they need to be taken to safety. If the victim has transportation, find out first if she is in condition to drive (victims not only suffer physically but also emotionally, and may be in no condition to drive).

7) Suggest safe places, making sure the abused person chooses a place (sometimes they know a safe place in a relative's home nearby, unknown to the abuser). Abuse agencies have several advantages over private homes. They have their own security, they are never alone; police officers cover them regularly and are on call. These agencies are usually hidden from the public.

8) Does the victim need medical care? Do any family members need medical attention or care? Some abuse civic agencies suggest that victims of abuse document and photograph physical evidence for their own protection later.

9) Victims of abuse need care and counseling to process the trauma of physical abuse to themselves and loved ones. Urge the parishioner to secure support and counseling for their distress. Remind them that there are several private and confidential places to get support without criminal investigation (abuse shelters will provide group and individual counseling whether a person presses charges or not). Remember that full-time employees of childcare centers, medical personnel, and government employees are required by certain states to report abuse and/or neglect. These "mandated reporters" include church employees operating licensed childcare facilities.

10) The average female victim returns to her spouse for at least four more violent episodes before she will leave him. Victims will try to talk

you into believing that the abuser has "repented" and "reformed" (the same comments the perpetrator has used).

11) Sometimes the church building may be used as the first "safe" place where the victim and authorities can meet. Most victims are afraid of involving police officers; they have often been beaten afterward by their spouse for "cooperating" with the police. Meeting in the church may alleviate some of these fears. Remember that we still call the worship center "the sanctuary" today, using a word from centuries ago when people who feared for their lives could run to a religious property to ask for protection from harm.

12) Children are especially vulnerable to physical harm, and most states now have laws that protect children from abusive or neglectful parents. Child Protective Services can provide your church group with brochures that detail what is considered abusive or neglectful behavior. In Virginia (and a few other states), there is also a group called "Prevent Child Abuse."

13) Caregivers who work with abused children (and adults) often have to brace themselves to witness some of the evidence of abuse. Listening to abused people's stories can be traumatic, too. Set limits to what you can handle, and ask other caregivers to help—confidentially!

14) Because physically abused persons live in danger of being harmed (intentionally or not), we need to be careful not to push them to place themselves at further risk in trying to help them get away from abusive behavior. Always let the victim decide what plan they can handle— and how soon.

For further reading:
Gary Collins, ed., *Counseling for Family Violence and Abuse* (Waco TX: Word Books, 1987).

Kermeth J. Doka, *Disenfranchised Grief: Recognizing Hidden Sorrow* (Lexington MA: Lexington Books, 1989).

Andrew Lester, *Pastoral Care with Children in Crises* (Philadelphia: Westminster Press, 1983).

Sexual Abuse

1) Because sexual abuse has such negative (and legal) implications for abusers, vulnerable children and young people fear disclosing sexual abuse in their family more than any other form of abuse.

2) If a child or youth courageously calls for help, or mentions any inappropriate behavior by an adult, the first thing to do is to take the young person seriously and not dismiss their comment because "they are a child." Listen carefully and confidentially. There is no reason to overreact or to panic.

3) Treat comments about sexual behavior with as much discretion as possible. Ask the person if they have shared the information with anyone else. Secure their permission to share it with a pastor or trusted adult they know. Inquire as to whether a parent is aware of the behavior(s). Remember, however, that many spouses are aware of inappropriate sexual activity but choose to deny it in order to shield a family from investigation or embarrassment. Don't automatically trust a spouse's comments.

4) Young children often don't know how to explain or even understand sexual behaviors and acts from trusted adults; they often only consider the behaviors "wrong" if they are physically painful. If you suspect that a child is being sexually abused or molested, check with the pastor, or ask a childcare worker for help in how to approach the issue. Remember that Christ challenged us to protect children as vulnerable and trusting charges (Matthew 18:5-6), and he also asked us to be "wise as serpents and innocent as doves" (Matthew 10:16).

5) Excellent resources are available to help children report inappropriate sexual behavior. Always remember that our goal is to be redemptive and helpful to God's people; we want to protect children from inappropriate behaviors, and we want to help troubled adults seek help to curtail abusive behavior.

6) When children or youth have been molested, they may go to support groups for recovery and care. County and state agencies will tell you what is available in each community; community service centers also provide counseling in rural areas. Private counseling for victims of sexual abuse is another important option, and pastoral counseling centers with trained personnel are one of the best choices for this type of care.

7) As difficult as it may be to believe, there are a number of families who tolerate and ignore sexual misconduct within the family. Incestuous acts are not rare, and in a society where one family in four is a "blended" group of remarried adults housing children of former marriages, inappropriate and irresponsible sexual intimacies take place. Caring for such vulnerable and wounded people is our challenge, since we may be the only adults acting as their advocates.

For further reading:
Barbara Bean & Shari Bennett, *The Me Nobody Knows: A Guide for Teen Survivors* (San Francisco: Jossey-Bass, 1999).

Linda Goldman, *Breaking the Silence: A Guide to Help Children with Complicated Grief—Suicide, Homicide, AIDS, Violence, and Abuse* (New York: Accelerated Development, 1996).

Hagans & Case, *When Your Child Has Been Molested* (San Francisco: Jossey-Bass, 1988).

Andrew Lester, *When Children Suffer* (Philadelphia: Westminster, 1987).

Cynthia Mather & Kristina Debye, *How Long Does It Hurt?: A Guide to Recovering from Incest and Sexual Abuse for Teenagers* (San Francisco: Jossey-Bass, 1998).

Spiritual Abuse

1) Contrary to the popular notion that all religious experiences are good, there are abusive religious practices and behaviors, and you may be asked to intervene in a crisis involving inappropriate religious practices.

2) Some parents distort the biblical principle of "respect for parents" as freedom to impose unnecessary and irresponsible burdens upon their

children (Ephesians 6:4). Oppressed and abused children may be taught that any resistance to a parental demand is wrong, including sexual favors. Some children witness the beating of a parent (usually a mother) as a way to "make her submissive, as the Bible teaches."

3) Some spouses submit to irresponsible physical abuse, believing that their husbands have a right to punish them physically.

4) Some believers interpret passages such as Proverbs 13:24, "Those who spare the rod hate their children, but those who love them are diligent to discipline them," to mean that they should beat their children regularly. These believers forget that the "rod" referred to in the Scripture is the same tool used in Psalm 23:4, "thy rod and thy staff, they comfort me." The shepherd rod was for guiding and protecting, not beating sheep!

5) Children and women are most vulnerable to spiritual abuse, and physical signs of abuse, depression, emotional withdrawal, and unusual displays of fear (recurring tears) may be the only clues to oppressive behavior that we see.

6) As before, in the section on physical abuse, we recommend that you work with the church staff to move at-risk children and adults to safe places where a calmer evaluation of the situation can take place.

7) A pastor or skilled lay leader can help a parishioner understand that God never intended for people to be violated or abused (speaking to the victim), nor oppressed and mistreated in the name of family ties (speaking to the abuser).

8) The church can play an active role in heading off inappropriate and manipulative use of the Bible by teaching and preaching the gospel of love as modeled in the life of Christ, who treated children, women, and vulnerable human beings with special, gentle care.

9) Some people use religion to justify controlling and authoritarian behavior in families. They oppress and manipulate people for years to the point that their victims' spirits are crushed and their self-confidence killed. If someone calls you for help after realizing that they have been controlled irresponsibly in the name of religion, help them by telling them that you understand, and that there are some choices they can begin to make to protect themselves from such destructive relationships. Suggest that they talk with their pastor or a pastoral counselor first to gain perspective on the issue.

For further reading:
Cloud and Townsend, *Safe People* (Grand Rapids MI: Zondervan, 1996).

J. LeBron McBride, *Spiritual Crisis: Surviving Trauma to the Soul* (New York: The Haworth Press, 1998).

Walter Wink, *Engaging the Powers* (Philadelphia: Fortress Press, 1992).

Addiction

1) There are several kinds of addiction, and we focus here on drug dependence, whether physiological or psychological. (See Alcoholism separately.)

2) When a family member calls for help with addiction, be aware that they often feel helpless and need encouragement. Ask first what degree of danger the person may be in at the moment, because you may need to call for emergency medical assitance or police officers to intervene in a life-or-death situation. People on drugs can mistakenly overdose, take dangerous and unknown substances, or lose control of their faculties and place themselves in jeopardy. (Be sure to ask for a correct address and phone number.)

3) As soon as you know whether the person needs immediate help, listen to see if they are reaching out for help and need direction on which steps to take first. They may need to go to a hospital emergency room if the drugs are having a dangerous effect at the moment. They may be able to see their own doctor (if soon available) to begin the medical steps toward care, detoxification, and rehabilitation.

4) Some families don't want their own doctor involved. If you have time, ask the person if you may call them back. Check with your pastor or a trusted medical person you know for leads or references on medical personnel that can be of help to your parishioner. Churches and deacon groups would do well to have a short list of telephone numbers for medical emergencies.

5) Help the person (and the family) understand the importance of starting the help process, and assure them that there are people who can help them overcome even the heaviest addiction.

6) Remind the people whom you help that medical care and counseling will be needed for a period of time in order for rehabilitation to occur. They should be patient with themselves and not expect a complete solution right away.

7) Cost of rehabilitation and care may be an important factor in the person's response to a plan of recovery. Help them know that there are resources available to them, and check with your church leadership to make sure there is an established "benevolence fund" for such purposes. (Many churches take a "fifth Sunday" offering specifically for such needs.)

8) There are drug rehabilitation programs in and out of state, and addicted people can find as much privacy as they desire. Heavily addicted individuals may need to enter a resident facility where they can gain full-time care from a team of specialists trained to treat addiction.

9) Remember that addiction is a physiological or psychological dependence that probably has a neurological basis. It is not a matter of being "cured" by willpower, nor by prayer alone. Avoid judgmental and moralistic arguments with addicted people. Such talk only shames them, setting them up to feel inadequate, depressed, and more likely to seek additional drugs to "feel better."

10) Students of human behavior suggest that, at the core, all addictions are an inner craving to satisfy an unmet search for meaning. (See *Man's Search for Meaning* by Viktor Frankl, a Viennese psychiatrist [New York: Touchtone, 1962]).

For further reading:

Dennis C. Daley, *Kicking Addictive Habits Once & For All* (San Francisco: Jossey-Bass, 1998).

Harvey Milkman & Stanley Sunderwirth, *Craving Ecstasy: How Our Passions Become Addictions & What We Can Do* (San Francisco: Jossey-Bass, 1999).

Oliver J. Morgan & Merle Jordan, *Addiction and Spirituality* (St. Louis: Chalice Press, 1999).

Dianne Doyle Pita, *Addictions Counseling* (New York: Crossroad, 1994).

Dennis L. Thombs, *Introduction to Addictive Behaviors* (New York: Guilford Publications, 1999).

Additional resources:

Narcotics Anonymous (NA)—a national help group

County and state drug rehabilitation programs

Attention Deficit Hyperactivity Disorder (ADHD)

1) The first signals of overactive behavior in a home can be the cause of much anxiety. Lately labeled Attention Deficit Hyperactivity Disorder, or ADHD, the symptoms are usually a combination of a short attention span, a tendency to move from one activity to another in quick succession, an inability to concentrate, impulsive behavior, and a tendency to move from thought to thought in a haphazard and inconsistent way.

2) Families managing such behaviors become stressed and overwhelmed. They need medical evaluation to determine if a child (or a child and an adult in the family) is struggling with this issue. School work and school reports often are the first sign that a child is having trouble concentrating or performing. Since there is likely a biological (inherited) component in ADHD, children with these symptoms often are living with a parent who also struggles with attention and activity issues.

3) Medication can help attention and behavior struggles, but families need to know that there is now some concern with overmedicating children. Ritalin, a popular medication in ADHD control, has been reported as a "wonder drug" in helping children concentrate in school. At the same time, it has been recorded as too quickly prescribed by physicians. Families stressed by hyperactive behavior need relief and support in the care of their children, but they also need perspective and wisdom in not relying too heavily on medication to control behaviors.

4) Sunday school teachers and other caregivers may be the first to report unusual behaviors in children. These observations need to be shared with parents. If you are the caregiver for a family dealing with hyperactivity issues, make sure you offer compassion and support for the entire family, since they must absorb some of the energy and intensity of this behavior.

5) Offer encouragement and help to the family and the person involved. Many families manage hyperactivity with a great deal of success, and two out of three children apparently can outgrow some of the symptoms of ADHD. Also assure that family members don't label a child (or an adult) too quickly as a "problem," and that the family undergoes regular medical evaluations in using any prescription medication for behavior control. Remind families, however, that like epilepsy, diabetes, high blood pressure, and other biological conditions, ADHD can be effectively monitored so that sufferers can lead productive lives.

6) When a child struggles with attention and behavior issues, make sure that teachers, deacons, and other people who have regular contact with the family are informed. Thus, the community of faith may participate in the care of family and person in a responsible way. Affecting about three percent of the population, ADHD appears more often in young boys, and it is biologically an unintentional set of behaviors. Don't punish children for not "paying attention" before you find out if they actually have the ability to do so.

For further reading:

Diane Ehrensaft, *Spoiling Childhood* (New York: Guilford Publications, 1999).

Russell A. Barkley, *Taking Charge of ADHD: A Complete, Authoritative Guide for Parents* (New York: Guilford, 2001).

David B. Stein, *Ritalin Is Not the Answer* (San Francisco: Jossey-Bass, 1999).

Aging

When you work with a family caring for aging parents who face changes, a few guidelines may be useful.

1) Suggest to family caregivers that they allow parents as much independence as they can handle. Every removed autonomous activity reduces freedom and self-esteem.

2) Prepare mature adults for major changes through a series of regular dialogues in which you explain why those changes need to take place. Listen to how they feel about the changes. Even those who face imminent change will adjust better with several opportunities to discuss their feelings. Be prepared for their grief over the closing of a chapter in their lives.

3) Suggest that family caregivers provide various options from which senior adults may choose (where possible). Choices extend independence and self-reliance. Make sure the available choices are clearly stated.

4) Where major changes are necessary, suggest that family caregivers invite/solicit the participation of family members. The gathered family symbolizes joint responsibility.

5) Encourage family members to review options and study available choices in independent living, nursing care, total care, critical care, hospitalization, finances, and insurance coverage. Consult on power of attorney needs.

6) Remind family caregivers that the senior adult and every family member involved with the senior adult are moving through a grief process, and that denial, depression, bargaining, anger, and cooperation are normal stages toward acceptance of change and loss.

7) Personal safety is a major issue. If driving, cooking, or living alone are no longer safe, suggest that trusted friends of the senior adult confirm the danger and advocate for reasonable changes. Ministers, nurses, police officers, doctors, and other authorities may be needed to convince a family member to disengage from an activity. Offer options if possible!

8) Encourage family caregivers to read materials on senility, Alzheimer's, and other possible developments in their family's life, so that they will understand when their parent or loved one undergoes personality changes or at times becomes verbally harsh.

9) Challenge family caregivers to exercise as much patience as possible, listening longer, expecting less, and adjusting to the loss of the parent as they knew them. Prepare them for the possibility of having to say goodbye gradually to a loved one who is only a shadow of the person they once knew. Remind them that their sadness is anticipated loss.

10) Energy and perspective are needed in the care of a parent. Help children who care for aging parents to understand how much emotional energy is consumed in caring, especially in their own home.

11) Make sure all who live in the family have been consulted before a senior adult is brought to live in the home, for the whole family system is traumatized under such circumstances.

12) Teach caregiving adult children how to rely on the church as a community of faith to offer activities and opportunities of service for a senior adult, support for the hosting family, and workshops in which all may be equipped and encouraged to make solid decisions based on protective love.

13) Point the family to (or form) a support group for children of institutionalized parents, so that they have a compassionate and understanding circle of friends with whom to meet regularly.

14) Watch family members who are primary caregivers for "compassion fatigue" (see **Compassion Fatigue**), the normal experience of becoming emotionally and physically exhausted during the extended care of a dependent. Help them find ways to rest and to distance themselves from the intensity of constant caregiving.

For further reading:

Michael Butler & Ann Orbach, *Being Your Age: Pastoral Care for Older People* (Perthshire England: Pioneer Associates, 1993).

Carol Dettoni, *Caring for Those Who Can't* (Wheaton IL: Victor Books, 1993).

Vivian E. Greenberg, *Respecting Your Limits When Caring for Aging Parents* (San Francisco: Jossey-Bass, 1989).

D.T. & Dudley Hall, *God's Care for Widows* (Euless TX: Titus Publishing, 1983).

Marlene Halpin, *Caregivers: Reflections on Coping with Caregiving* (Dubuque IA: Islewest Publishing, 1998).

Marlene Hunter, *Making Peace with Chronic Pain* (New York: Brunner/Mazel, 1998).

Henry C. Simmons & Mark A. Peters, *With God's Oldest Friends* (New York: Paulist Press, 1996).

Additional resources:

Alzheimer's Disease & Related Disorders (1-800-621-0379)

Children of Aging Parents (org.) in Levittown, Pennsylvania

National Council on the Aging, Washington, D.C., which offers a free listing of publications on aging (202-479-1200)

AIDS

1) Our society is still poorly educated on Acquired Immune Deficiency Syndrome (AIDS), a human condition in which the body loses its capacity to fight most kinds of diseases, leaving its victim defenseless against almost every infection. Human Immunodeficiency Virus (HIV) is the viral complex that causes AIDS. AIDS is the resulting syndrome created by HIV's depletion of the body's immune system.

2) If a church member calls you and declares that they are afraid they have HIV or AIDS, your first question should probably be if they have been tested for infectious diseases or seen by a doctor. A common myth about HIV is that it can be contracted by anyone who has minimal contact with an HIV-positive or AIDS-infected person. The only known way that someone can become infected with HIV is by direct contact of internal bodily fluids between persons (such as a blood transfusion, exchange of fluids during sexual intercourse, sharing of a syringe or needle infected by a carrier, ingestion of the breast milk of an infected person, etc.). In other words, AIDS can only be transmitted through blood, reproductive fluids or breast milk.

3) Families of infected individuals are often afraid and feel helpless. They need as much ministering as a victim of HIV/AIDS. Although until recently victims expected an early death, improved medications and better health practices have prolonged life and extended hope for AIDS patients.

4) Families of infected people need education and understanding; they also need level-headed friends who will help them maintain perspective and who will not withdraw from them physically, emotionally, or spiritually. You can help such traumatized people by helping other church members understand the condition of someone with AIDS. The sick person is not a "carrier" who can infect other people through simple, day-to-day contact. The AIDS patient also needs help in educating church members on how they can best minister to him or her.

5) Some church members may have been infected with HIV because of a blood transfusion that was not adequately screened. Unfortunately, such people have often been discriminated against and stereotyped in some congregations as if they were sexually promiscuous or irresponsible. A ministry of care for these wounded members involves advocating for them and educating the church to which they belong.

6) Remember that AIDS/HIV victims often become quite depressed and may call you with destructive—and sometimes suicidal— thoughts. Listen attentively to a depressed person, and acknowledge their feelings and concerns. Help them understand that they are valued as friends and family members, and that there can be hope for their medical condition. Be careful, however, about causing false hopes. It is best to assure that the patient sees a doctor and then to support the patient during treatment. Ask patients what their doctor has told them; find out how their family is responding. Ask: "What right now is most depressing to you?" Ask also: "Are you in immediate danger of harming yourself?" If they are in danger, you should get them to a safe place (often an Emergency Room in a local hospital) where they can be medicated and monitored. (See **Suicide** if you suspect heavy depression.)

7) Make sure depressed individuals are not alone. If a depressed person calls and tells you that they don't care if they live anymore, ask to speak to a housemate or family member. Find out if the family needs guidance in getting help. You may need to call authorities for them.

The local police department, in most places, is trained to respond as quickly as paramedics. They should be considered your second source of emergency help.

8) It's not necessary to keep promises of confidentiality when dealing with a suicidal person (see **Suicide**). We usually tell suicidal persons that we won't keep their secret (suicidal thoughts) if they are in danger of harming themselves. I'd rather have a live church member who is angry with me for breaking a confidence than a dead member whose confidentiality I honored . . . wouldn't you?

9) Use your doctors and other health officials in your church as sources of education and care for your congregation, and check with your pastor to build compassionate support for the victim of AIDS and his or her family.

For further reading:
Linda Goldman, *Breaking the Silence: A Guide to Help Children with Complicated Grief—Suicide, Homicide, AIDS, Violence* (New York: Taylor & Francis, 1996).

Alcoholism

1) If you get an emergency call to aid a family struggling with alcohol abuse, you might first check with your pastor (or a deacon with a history in the church) to learn more about this family's history with the abuse—and what has been done in the past to help them (it may save you time and unnecessary mistakes).

2) When you are called by a family member for help because someone in the family is out of control due to alcohol use, be careful to offer support without overextending yourself. Alcoholics cannot quit their addiction by simply using enough willpower or prayer. Shaming or moralizing an alcoholic does little but exact promises from them that they cannot keep. They need treatment and medical care, and the family needs to learn how to help them recover by supporting them but not making decisions for them.

3) We now know enough about alcoholism to understand that we are not caring for an individual addiction problem, but a family issue. We also know that there is a physiological predisposition to addiction and that alcoholism is a disease, not just a "poor habit" some people choose.

4) The safety of the family and the alcoholic is of first importance. People under the influence of alcohol lose perspective and judgment and can accidentally injure themselves or someone else. Ask the family what they need, but remember the following safety questions. Is anyone in danger of physical assault? Are there any weapons in the house? (Make sure they are not available to disoriented people.) Is

someone planning to drive a car under the influence? Does the drinker
need to be transported to an institution for care? (Resist the idea of a
family member—or you—transporting an inebriated person by themselves in a car; it's not safe.)

5) Will the drinker respond to one particular person more than
another (pastor, friend, etc.) and follow their suggestions for safety and
stability? If so, gain permission for that person to visit as soon as possible to help the family regain some balance. The active alcoholic
upsets the balance in a family and attracts a good portion of time and
energy when "in a crisis." Family members grow weary of rescuing or
covering for the drinker and need care themselves.

6) Victims of alcoholism never stop being alcoholics; they learn to set
controls over the addiction through a disciplined (and difficult) recovery process that requires their complete avoidance of the substance. If
not, they will lose control over their lives.

7) Several organizations can help the alcoholic set and maintain controls. Alcoholics Anonymous is a group of recovering addicts who
meet weekly, often in churches, to give each other encouragement and
accountability. There are county and state detoxification programs
with group experiences and professional help for alcoholics. There are
also Brief Therapy Family Centers that offer short-term rehabilitation
that is often less expensive.

8) If you have an opportunity to discuss with an alcoholic his or her
options for getting help, remember the following tips:

• The recovery program must be important to the drinker to work.
• The goals set must be small in order for the patient to succeed.
• Steps must be specific, dealing with behaviors.
• Goals should be set in positive ways—not just avoidance.
• The plan should be a beginning, not an end.
• Goals must be achievable, not enormous fantasies.
• The rehabilitation process will require hard work.

9) Families of problem drinkers need support and training, too. Alcoholics Anonymous offers group events for spouses (Al-Anon), and for teenagers (Al-Ateen). Other agencies also offer group care to help family members learn how to avoid contributing to the problem.

10) Remember that problem drinkers often struggle with issues such as control of impulsive behavior, physical or emotional abuse, and other concerns that may be unrelated to the alcohol addiction. They may need therapy and care to manage a variety of challenges. They and their loved ones need long-term care to survive as a family.

For further reading:
Insoo K. Berg & Scott Miller, *Working with the Problem Drinker* (New York: Norton, 1992).

Peter Steinglass, *The Alcoholic Family* (New York: Basic Books, 1987).

Anger

Someone may call for help because they are experiencing frustration, anger, and turmoil and aren't sure how to handle it. The following facts and advice about anger may help.

The Appearance of Anger

1) *Anger as Tears:* Some people have only been given permission to cry when they are angry.

2) *Anger as Explosion:* Some people vent their anger immediately and directly, often expecting to be rejected or to "distance" people.

3) *Indirect Anger:* Some people use anger in passive-aggressive ways, working "around" people and behind their backs. Usually afraid to confront their own anger, they often deny it exists.

4) *Anger as Depression:* Some folks "swallow" their anger and deal with the pain of anger turned upon themselves. They are usually afraid of their strong feelings.

5) *Anger as Withdrawal:* Some people choose to handle their anger by pulling away from a relationship, by becoming marginal and uninvolved.

6) *Projected or Displaced Anger:* Sometimes anger stemming from one relationship/event is carried over and vented in another relationship/event in which it seems "safer" to vent.

7) *Anger as Rejection:* Some people try to alleviate their anger by rejecting the person or experience that "caused" it. They refuse to deal with either one and usually choose not to talk about it, possibly hoping the pain will go away.

8) *Denial by Humor:* Although humor can diffuse anger, some people use humor as a way of disguising or totally denying the angry feelings they have. Hiding/denying anger can result in physical symptoms such as colitis, ulcers, indigestion, migraine headaches, etc.

Biblical Reasons for Anger

1) *Reaction to Manipulation:* Christ was angry with the Pharisees for such tactics (Matthew 22:18).

2) *Response to Abuse:* Anger is a caring response to the abuse of people; it is intended to control or stop such behavior (John 2:13-18).

3) *Anger as Care:* We become incensed because we care about something or someone (God did as well; Exodus 32:9-19).

4) *Anger as Grief:* We respond with deep feeling to a major loss over which we have no control (Job 3:1-26).

Redemptive Options for Anger

1) Help a parishioner identify and acknowledge the feelings and not deny them.

2) Remind them that anger itself is not sin, but it becomes sin if used in destructive ways.

3) Confess inappropriate wants, thoughts, hopes, actions. Confession cleanses, assumes responsibility, and acknowledges truth.

4) Focus on the reason(s) for the feelings. Some may be appropriate.

5) Don't ignore or reject the relationship. Deal with the issue, separating it from the person. Acknowledge pain and resistance.

6) Take initiative to clarify your responsibility in an event. Invite the other person to dialogue, and work to solve the problem and alleviate anger.

7) Ask a third party to listen and assist if you feel vulnerable.

8) Be the first person to ask for forgiveness, and wait for a response.

9) Assume only your responsibility in an issue; remember that reconciliation involves a willingness of both parties to forgive.

10) Pray throughout the process for openness, insight, perspective, peace, and grace.

For further reading:

Daniel G. Bagby, *Understanding Anger in the Church* (Nashville: Broadman Press, 1979).

Harriet G. Lerner, *The Dance of Anger* (New York: Harper & Row, 1985).

Birth Defects

1) When a newborn is diagnosed with a disability, inform the family of the spiritual and emotional care available to them as they face this news. Some parents feel the need to mask their disappointment and anger by rushing to the interpretation that their child's disability is a "blessing" from God. Give them permission to express their stunned sorrow and anger about their child's diagnosis. Burying anger only makes it stronger. There will be time later for adjustment and for finding a blessing.

2) Help the family gain access to professionals who can give them insight into the disability and help them assess if they can manage the child at home now, at some point in the future, or never. Some severe disabilities require permanent institutionalization.

3) Give the parents time to make their decisions, since the implications of each choice may mean a change for a lifetime.

4) Help the family gain access to community and financial resources that can assist them in the care of the child. Among the issues they will face are requirements for home care, potential hospital care, chances of the child's survival, and training in order to act as effective caregivers.

5) Teach parents of disabled infants that they do not have to choose between loving their child and experiencing the grief that naturally results from such major changes. They may grieve what they have lost (a normal infancy), and still love the unique child they have. Help them understand grief.

6) There are support groups for parents of children permanently disabled; check your county service agency for schedules and details. Remind the parents that they will experience "care exhaustion" (see **Compassion Fatigue**) and need relief and rest from the constancy of caregiving.

7) Parents of disabled infants sometimes think God is punishing them with the blemished birth. If you sense that a parishioner struggles with such an issue, suggest that they spend time exploring their feelings with the pastor or a pastoral counselor who can help them sort difficult feelings.

8) Make sure that you (or another caregiver) encourage the family with a disabled child to discuss together the impact the new birth will have on the family. Sometimes parents assume that they are absorbing all the work and stress involved in rearing a special child, but the reality is that the entire family is deeply affected by the addition and will not be the same again. Siblings of the disabled child need to understand the adjustments they are asked to make.

For further reading:
Bette M. Ross, *Our Special Child* (Nashville: Thomas Nelson, 1993).

Nancy L. Eiesland, *The Disabled God* (Nashville: Abingdon Press, 1994).

Death and Dying

1) One of the solemn crises of living is facing one's own death. When people know that they are dying, and have time to reflect on it, they need help in processing the reality of their approaching death. They and their families need help learning how to manage the loss.

2) Sometimes death is sudden, and the family has no time to antici-pate the loss. They deal with grief (see **Grief**), a subject approached elsewhere in this guide. But how do we help the person who is coming to terms with his or her own death?

3) People who anticipate dying usually want to talk about it, want help saying goodbye to loved ones, and want to see that their loved ones get help working through the loss.

4) Contrary to the notion that we help dying people by avoiding the subject of death, we help people most when we give them permission to talk about their own death. Whether at home or in the hospital, people who are dying have a need to evaluate, reflect, and give closure to life as they enter it final stages.

5) Elizabeth Kubler-Ross, a caregiver and student of issues surround-ing dying persons since 1967, spent a lot of time learning from dying people about their journey toward death. She identified five major issues or stages most people go through in this process. Those who are dying usually struggle first with *denial,* then *depression* (see **Depression**); then they try to *bargain,* eventually *deal with anger* (see **Anger**), and finally *accept* the reality of dying. You can be of help to

the parishioner and the family by understanding these normal reactions to the news of impending death.

6) Help the family understand how important it is for a terminally ill person to express his or her thoughts and feelings about dying. You may discover that a family member finds it too difficult to listen to their loved one's comments at any given time. Allow them to avoid the conversation if they choose, and encourage the dying person to share thoughts and feelings with another family member and with you and other caregivers. Tell them also the truth: they must come to terms with the reality of death, and it will help them, not hinder them, to talk about dying.

7) The first assistance a helper can provide a terminally ill parishioner in early conversations is to help them begin to accept the reality of their condition. Denial and unreality distract a person in the early stages of dealing with such stunning news. Asking the parishioner to repeat or explain what the doctor has told them is a good way to help the reality "sink in." Several conversations may be necessary for such painful news to be registered in the parishioner's mind.

8) If a person who has just learned that they are dying calls you and wants to talk about their anger, frustration, fear, and pain, listen to them. If they express anger at a God who would allow such dreadful things to happen, don't argue with them, but acknowledge their right to feel angry and to struggle with the fact of dying. There will be other occasions to "talk theology" with them.

9) Avoid making superficial comments that don't help the dying person and are usually made only to calm our own anxiety. Statements such as "God has a purpose in all this," "Let's not question God's will," "Someday all of this will make sense," and "I understand how you feel" are of little use to terminal patients.

10) People who are dying usually want to discuss their funeral arrangements, the distribution of their property, the writing of a living will,

and the legal preparation of a last will. Family members may choose to be involved in any of these conversations, but give them freedom to abstain if they feel unable to do so. Pastors are honored to help a person with funeral service plans. Some congregations have lawyers who volunteer their time to help prepare legal documents for a family.

11) If a person asks for a living will to be developed, they are usually referring to making their intentions clear in regard to medical procedures that might keep them alive artificially. DNR is a common acronym that means "Do Not Resuscitate," which some dying individuals want clearly understood in case they are unconscious and lose vital capacities (the ability to breathe on their own, maintain feeding, etc.). If at all possible, family members and the dying person should discuss these issues with each other. Understanding a person's wishes ahead of time avoids later distress and anguish (see **Right to Die Questions**).

12) Another important reason for encouraging the patient and family to talk together is that people's anxieties, concerns, and guilt can get resolved in the clarity of final conversations. Some of these sacred moments become significant opportunities for the expression of forgiveness, understanding, and love. For Christians, it can also become a wonderful experience of celebrating the dying person's life and contributions while the person can still understand and recognize the affirmations. The truest words stated to a dying man by a thief on a cross next to him were words of deep affirmation: "for we are getting what we deserve for our deeds, but this man has done nothing wrong . . . . Jesus, remember me when you come into your kingdom" (Luke 23:41b-42).

13) Remember that the end of life can be a time of gratitude and remembrance and a unique opportunity to celebrate a rich human journey well lived. Many older people receive the news of a terminal condition with positive perspective, and some even feel relief, especially if they have been suffering physically or emotionally. Like Simeon in the temple at the sight of the infant Jesus, some senior

adults feel that they have completed their heart's desire at a certain point in old age and are ready to die (Luke 2:26-29). Paul himself came to a point where he looked forward to death (2 Timothy 4:6-8).

14) The Hospice program now available in many communities is a caregiving ministry for people who are dying. Hospice agents usually work with a family and patient during the last six months of the patient's life, after all procedures for healing or recovery have been exhausted. A team of caregivers usually consists of nurses, social workers, spiritual directors (chaplains), caregiving volunteers, and medical consultants. The patient often is cared for in their own home as long as possible, and the medication provided is mostly for the control of pain (palliative measures). A family may request this type of care if available. There is a cost for the program.

15) You may lead your church in preparing for the reality of death, since no institution deals with death in a more hopeful or caring way. There are materials and journals that focus entirely on what is called "death education" (thanatology), not from a morbid point of view, but in order to educate and prepare children, youth, and adults for this inevitable and transforming event.

For further reading:
Elisabeth Kubler-Ross, *On Death & Dying* (New York: The Macmillan Co., 1969).

Betty Davies et al., eds., *Fading Away: The Experience of Transition in Families with Terminal Illness* (New York: Baywood Publishing, 2000).

Peck & Stefanics, *Learning to Say Goodbye* (Muncie IN: Accelerated Development Inc., 1987).

Froma Walsh & Monica McGoldrick, eds., *Living Beyond Loss: Death in the Family* (New York: W.W. Norton, 1991).

When a Death Occurs

The following guidelines can help if you are called to respond to a death in your church family while the pastor is out of town.

1) If the death is sudden and you are involved in telling the family, plan so that family members are not alone when told. Family, friends, neighbors are of great support for providing details and helping with chores.

2) Consider these questions when determining the best way to help.

- Are there family members and special friends who need to be notified? Should someone drive them home?
- Is someone (not family) available to answer the phone at the home of the deceased?
- Can meals be prepared and synchronized so that all food does not arrive the same day?
- Do children need to be picked up at school or located and cared for?
- Do certain responsibilities need to be cancelled or assumed by others?
- Can someone keep a record of visitors, flowers, and gifts of food?
- Have arrangements previously been made with a specific funeral home? Are there plans for a service that need to be carried out? Did the deceased or family members want a memorial service in the church worship center? The funeral home? A graveside service? Do plans involve choosing a casket? Cremation? Are there insurance papers/legal papers that need to go to a funeral home meeting? Have family members chosen pallbearers, if they so desire?
- Does the family want the minister to go to the funeral home with them (usually by appointment)? Is the funeral home personnel attentive to the wishes of the family?
- How is the funeral service to be structured? (Provide guidance, but be sensitive to family desires.) Is there a special solo (music) desired? Are there hymns of choice? Any Scriptures that are special to family/deceased? Any poems or proverbs that have been associated

with the deceased? Are there any particular individuals the family wants involved in the service? Any family members who wish to be involved?

• Is any unique organization involved in the funeral service (Masonic Lodge, military rituals, organizations, etc.)? Understand their part in the service, especially at the graveside.

3) Help the family consider regional and family traditions in regard to open-casket services, viewing the body, etc. Visit the family at their home (if possible) in order to plan the service with them. Be prepared to offer suggestions in regard to Scriptures, hymns, order of worship, length of the service, etc.

4) The content of a funeral service should acknowledge the reality of death, the sorrow of separation, the presence of God, the assurance of God's love, the gift of a person's life, and the certainty of the resurrection. Affirmations about God's gift of life in the power of human love, God's comfort in loss, and God's gift of eternal life are powerful expressions of the good news without coming across as overly evangelistic. An evangelistic sermon is both unnecessary and largely inappropriate at a funeral! Begin your preparation of a personal eulogy by asking family members to tell you about the qualities of their loved one that most impressed them, qualities that live on because they shared them. Use those comments in a brief affirmation of the deceased's life.

5) A worship service at a church building is most effective if no more than a thirty-minute event; in a funeral parlor, twenty to twenty-five minutes is ideal. If you are one of two or more ministers, don't "preach" if someone already has! The emotional energy of a grieving family is severely taxed. Why wear them down with a long, drawn out service? Remember that they still have to go to a gravesite then to visit for several hours with family and friends, some of whom traveled to attend the funeral.

6) Instead of going to the family home after the graveside service, let the family visit with each other without you. Call the immediate family in the next day or two, then visit them in a few days. Your timely visit means more after a few days than right after the funeral when the mourners are numb and overextended.

7) Following is a preferred order of funeral service with many church members.

Prelude
Solo (usually someone the family feels close to, or a song loved by family)
Statement of Purpose/Reading of Obituary/Family Information
Scripture Reading (Psalms/Isaiah/Gospels/Paul's Letters)
Pastoral Prayer
Solo
Eulogy/Brief Homily
Benediction (remain at head of casket while family is escorted)

8) Graveside services (where service has preceded the interment) are intended to be brief. They are simply a reminder of God's love and care, a brief Scripture reading, and a closing prayer. If graveside is the only service, include a possible solo, the reading of the obituary (family information), and a brief homily. Ask the family about their preferences.

9) Funeral homes can be a genuine ally to ministers and family. They make all arrangements for the removal of a body (from home, hospital, or morgue), arrange for services in other towns, transport family, oversee flower arrangements, provide newspaper with information, call pallbearers and ministers, prepare guest books, provide flags (military), make all arrangements with special organizations, arrange funeral plot and funeral escort, and provide music as desired. Most directors are sincere and helpful.

10) Presiding at a funeral worship service is a sacred privilege. If you have been asked to do so, consider it an honor and set aside your fears

of inadequacy. The family may need your leadership and your quiet direction.

Complicated/Sudden Loss

1) Several losses in the course of living are unacknowledged, complicated, unresolved, or unidentified because they are either disguised, gradual, ignored, or misunderstood. A parishioner may call you in the sudden awareness of a deep and confusing general sorrow. Some of our most common unacknowledged losses are:

• a broken relationship (including an interrupted engagement).
• belief crisis: losing foundational faith beliefs or values.
• development of a disabling disease (multiple sclerosis, Alzheimer's).
• geographic move.
• identity loss: losing an image we've long held of ourselves.
• role change: losing a title or position in a social group.

2) Several other unacknowledged losses have been treated separately in this guide (**Abuse**, **Aging**, **Infertility/Miscarriage**, **Mental Illness**, **Rape**, etc.).

3) People juggling complicated losses need care through several experiences. Early stages include disbelief, confusion, detachment, and numbness.

4) Intermediate responses include sadness, disorganization, yearning, resentment, embarrassment, fatigue, restlessness, and anxiety about the future.

5) Culminating responses occur later and involve a reorganization and reconnection that gives the parishioner a new definition of their identity and future. Help the church member recognize and process each of these emotional/spiritual journeys by explaining them along the way.

6) When a parishioner begins to understand that they are in a period of bereavement, suggest resources in the church and community that will assist them to identify the unacknowledged loss, understand more about its impact, and adjust to the loss by shaping a modified sense of themselves and their future.

7) Grieving parishioners often need to work through reevaluated spiritual struggles that may include anger at God, disbelief and detachment, reorganization of their belief system, and a reconnecting with God under different expectations. Help them find pastoral leadership for such conversations. Guide them to people who will not make them feel punished or condemned for struggling with doubt and anger. Note how many times the psalmists shared both feelings with God— Psalms 22, 38, 74, 88, etc.

For further reading:

Daniel G. Bagby, *Seeing Through Our Tears: Why We Cry/How We Heal* (Minneapolis: Augsburg, 1999).

Kenneth Mitchell & Herbert Anderson, *All Our Losses, All Our Griefs: Resources for Pastoral Care* (Philadelphia: The Westminster Press, 1983).

Roslyn Karaban, *Complicated Losses, Difficult Deaths* (San Jose CA: Resource Publishing Inc., 2000).

Therese A. Rando, *Treatment of Complicated Mourning* (Champaign IL: Research Press Co., 1993).

Right to Die Questions

1) Parishioners and their families sometimes face the difficult decision of choosing whether or not to discontinue treatments, comfort-maintenance medications, and life-sustaining procedures.

2) The patient's will is of primary interest in regard to continuing treatments. As long as a patient is conscious and can make their own decisions, they have the right to vote on any interventions that may cause suffering and/or produce short extensions of life. Suggest a "family council" in which family members are coached on listening to each other with respect and dignity and listening to a patient's point of

view. Family members can be selfish about wanting to have a dying relative extend their life, often at the cost of much pain and misery to everyone involved, claiming that it is for the sake of the family.

3) Doctors can help family members understand the options and value of administering medication that reduces the dying parishioner's pain. Unless there are significant personal beliefs that prohibit the patient from receiving such medications (palliative measures), encourage the parishioner and the family to accept or continue such care. This provides quality time, and shields the patient and the family from unncessary pain. Physical and emotional pain sap energy from a patient, reducing their endurance.

4) What about choices to discontinue life-support equipment? Remember that each state has laws interpreting some of these decisions; help your parishioner and family access that information unless it is already clear.

5) The family and the patient (if possible) should also discuss this issue so that family members understand the patient's wishes, and so that everyone involved has a clear understanding of what each believes and can choose to do.

6) The issue of pain and misery is of first consideration to many families, and deciding what to do about comfort medication may resolve all the choices that a family and dying loved one may believe they can make.

7) Some hospitals (especially church-owned institutions) may also have guidelines that set limits on what procedures or interruption of procedures will be allowed. Check to see if the family you are serving understands what the hospital and law restrictions are. Many hospitals have Ethics Boards that have defined what constitutes "active" and "inactive" interventions in regard to the introduction or removal of life-support systems.

8) A family should always be informed of the decisions undertaken by the hospital personnel. Ask the family what they have been told, and check to see if there is clarity or confusion. Sometimes confusing terms used by nurses and doctors make decisions more difficult.

9) Make sure that clergy (chaplains) or skilled pastoral counselors attend the family's needs when questions about discontinuing life-support systems are addressed. Guilt and sadness often accompany such tough decisions; reassure family members of God's grace and compassion in all such delicate decisions.

10) Some terms like "physician-assisted suicide" are unfortunate and highly suggestive. Suicide is not a "neutral" word to many people. Thus, this term needs to be used appropriately and cautiously. If a parishioner wants to talk with you about their struggle over medical interventions that would accelerate their death, listen caringly and compassionately. Make sure you've prayed about the issue because your values will surface. Note: Many medical personnel believe that offering Jesus Christ vinegar at the cross was a procedure to alleviate his pain and hasten his death.

11) The right to die "with dignity" is an appropriate and frequently discussed issue. Make sure the patient and the family (where possible) have access to responsible religious conversations on their options and the choices they decide to make. Pray with them as they seek God's will in this matter; help them sense the presence of God in their delicate choices.

12) Families face difficult questions during these times. Be sensitive to questions like the following. The advance of science has made it possible to maintain "life" artificially for extended periods of time. Is such artificial maintenance always God's will? Is maintenance of a "vegetative state" (no brain activity) over a long period of time life as God intended it? At what point in the loss of bodily functions does a human being (or a family) have the responsibility or right to discontinue artificial procedures? Does a parishioner ever have the right to

accelerate their own physical death by artificial means in order to avoid extended pain to themselves and their family?

13) Such questions will emerge frequently in parishioners' minds in times of crisis. They need the caring and compassionate guidance of clergy, communities of faith, and responsible professionals to help them with answers. Congregations can address these issues in workshops, seminars, and other open conversations as a ministry to the people of God facing a new day in medical capabilities.

For further reading:
Joyce Ashton & Dennis Ashton, *Loss and Grief Recovery: Help Caring for Children with Disabilities, Chronic or Terminal Illness* (Amityville NY: Baywood Publishing, 2000).

Kalman J. Kaplan, ed., *Right to Die Versus Sacredness of Life* (Amityville NY: Baywood, 1999).

David Wendell Moller, *On Death Without Dignity: The Human Impact of Technological Dying* (Amityville NY: Baywood, 2000).

Stillbirth

1) When a family or friend calls with news of a stillbirth, remember to treat it as a death experience in the family. Stillbirth is a complicated, sometimes unacknowledged event.

2) If the family is still in the hospital, make sure (with their permission) that a pastor and, if available, a sensitive best friend inquire about the possibility of visiting.

3) Death at birth is the reversal of one of life's greatest joyful expectations—the gift of a baby—into a stunning intrusion of emptiness and loss.

4) Sometimes the family wants privacy at first. If so, you may help by conveying that message to friends and church family. A sign on a door, a message on an answering machine, or a friend standing at the door with a note pad to record messages of care can assist the family in securing privacy in their time of grief.

5) It should be obvious that the loss of a baby at birth is a major bereavement, but you may want to remind family members gently that they have the right to feel numb, stunned, depressed, emotional, angry, and confused with the sudden and traumatic reversal of their anticipated joy.

6) Spouses often feel helpless and disoriented and may need guidance in making impending decisions. Does the family wish to have a burial service, a memorial service, or a quiet family ceremony? They have the right to choose as they wish, but they may be so stunned that the decision should be postponed until a more appropriate time. Have other children in the family been informed? What about out-of-town family members who have been awaiting good news? Does the wife need to remain in the hospital for further care? The hospital may ask if the family desires an autopsy, or they may ask permission to perform one. These decisions belong to the parents but may require processing and evaluation under stress. Help, but don't interfere.

7) Help the church (and the family) organize gestures of care. Food brought to the home should not all arrive on the same day. Is there a deacon group assigned to coordinate such a schedule? Childcare (if needed) could be coordinated. Children, absorbing the family stress, need as little change in their routine as possible. Can someone answer the phone when the family needs rest and protection from repeated explanations? Sometimes a church office can coordinate these needs and others as they emerge.

8) Are there chores or errands that you (or another caregiver) can perform to reduce the strain of "maintenance" details for the family? Is transportation for various family members of help?

9) You can also provide assistance (as pastor or layperson) by rehearsing a comment that can be shared with a church family (either at the church office, at a prayer meeting, or on a recorded message) that can save energy and interpretation for family members who have to "field" phone calls for the next few days.

10) At an appropriate time, suggest that counseling (and perhaps a grief support group) may be of strength and sustenance in the recovery process that takes several months, and sometimes years. Resist giving medical advice to the couple about future pregnancies, but refer them to their doctors and counselors.

11) Normal grief reaction to a stillborn birth involves wondering where God was in the event and feeling angry at God for the loss. These responses are normal experiences after a death, and listening to and acknowledging the pain and frustration of the loss is your most helpful contribution. Say, "Your sorrow and disappointment have to be great. I'm so sorry." Avoid saying, "I understand how you feel" (unless you've also lost a child at birth), or "you'll have another child someday, I just know it"(you can't possibly know this). Acknowledge their sorrow. Don't try to cheer them up right away; allow them time to grieve this significant and painful loss.

For further reading:

Kenneth J. Doka, ed., *Grief After Sudden Loss* (New York: Taylor & Francis, 1994).

Roslyn Karaban, *Complicated Losses, Difficult Deaths: A Practical Guide for Ministering to Grievers* (San Jose CA: Resource Publications, Inc., 2000).

Therese A. Rando, *Treatment of Complicated Mourning* (Champaign IL: Research Press Co., 1993).

Depression

1) More than twenty million Americans experience depression at some point in their lives. What psychiatrists usually call a "mood disorder," depression can occur with high and low mood swings, as in bi-polar disorder, or with recurring bouts of mainly low mood swings, which are usually referred to as major depressions.

2) When a parishioner calls in a state of depression, your greatest gift to them is the labor of patient listening. Depressed people quickly lose perspective, and one of the first conclusions they reach is that no one cares for them and that they are on their own.

3) It is important to ask the depressed person if he or she is on medication and is taking the recommended dose. Depressed people frequently either quit taking their medication or begin taking too much. Find out if they are seeing a doctor or a psychiatrist, the only kind of mental health therapist who has a medical degree and can prescribe medication.

4) When severely depressed, parishioners often have an agreement with their doctor or psychiatrist that permits a phone call to the doctor to evaluate whether an increased dosage of medicine will help them. As ministering caregivers, we don't have the power to make those decisions. We should always encourage patients to call their doctor and discuss the issue with the trained professional.

5) Depressed people often have impaired judgment and don't make decisions wisely. We can help as we listen to them by assuring that

they are not making major decisions while depressed (quitting a job, leaving a spouse, leaving town, selling the house, harming themselves, etc.). People who are severely depressed should not be left alone, and they sometimes need to be hospitalized for their own protection.

6) Be alert for these signs of deep depression: inability to sleep or sleeping too much, loss of appetite and/or weight loss, irritable and anxious mood, loss of energy, loss of interest in activities, limited ability to concentrate, feelings of worthlessness, physical aches or pains, recurring thoughts of harming oneself (suicidal), racing thoughts, rapid speech while in a high mood, slurred/slow speech while in a low mood, sense of hopelessness about changing and getting better, etc.

7) Depressed people often talk to themselves, repeating a number of inaccurate ideas. A sample of poor thinking patterns:

"Everyone is adjusting to our work schedule but me." This is universal thinking, as if "everyone" in the office had been evaluated.
"No one seems to have trouble with relationships except me." This is negative universal error, believing that they are the only person having trouble getting along with some people.
"I never do anything right." This is maximizing a single mistake so that it appears to happen all the time.
"Sure I prepared the report well, but anyone could have done it as well." This is minimizing one's own contribution.

To help a depressed parishioner, listen for such words as "never," "always," and other words that exaggerate a condition. Then challenge that misperception by pointing it out to the discouraged person.

8) Listen for the above signals of depression, and find out if the depressed person is capable of regaining perspective. They may simply need solid attention and care for a few minutes on the phone. However, they may require intervention and perhaps hospitalization due to strong depressive thoughts.

9) Ask if the person is alone. A family member may be more anxious than the depressed person about their condition and may wonder what to do. With deeply troubled people, ask direct questions. There is no harm in saying the word "suicide" to a depressed person; they've probably already thought about it. "Have you been thinking about hurting yourself, John?" or "Mary, tell me how much you've thought about suicide during this low time." "Tell me, Jim, has taking your own life been on your mind during this time of depression?" The fact that you say the words helps a parishioner know that you can listen to their worst fears and get them help. "If you've been wondering about whether you wanted to end it all, I want to make sure we get you help so you can be cared for. We can take you to a hospital or doctor's office where you don't need to fight this pain all by yourself. I want you to stay alive; this is the wrong time to make big decisions about your life."

10) Sometimes a parishioner has waited so late to call that they are in critical need of help. If they are alone, ask them to stay put while you get help. Many depressed individuals don't truly wish to die; they simply don't know what to do when they've run out of options to stop the emotional pain they feel. Call 911 immediately, unless you have quick access to nearby emergency paramedics. The police departments in many communities have been trained for emergency responses, and the dispatch service for 911 calls may be the fastest response to life-and-death situations.

11) If you live near the depressed person and know there will be a waiting period for help to arrive, assign the emergency call to someone else, and tell the parishioner that you are on your way to their house. Sometimes a distraught person will postpone harming themselves if they know someone is coming to help.

12) If you can, exact a promise from a depressed parishioner that they will make no decisions to harm themselves until you or help arrives. Push them to promise that they will wait. Even your intensity will show that you care.

13) Remember that we can do our best to try to keep a distraught person from harming themselves, but we cannot be responsible for their choices. Some people call us when it is too late to help; some people harm themselves by accident, seeking help in a damaging way. Some people have hurt so long that they only want relief from their misery and try to end the pain by killing themselves.

14) Don't care for depressed people by yourself. We need the support and nurture of the community of faith to journey through many difficult experiences, and depression and suicide are two of the worst (see **Suicide** for more information). Call a pastor (or a colleague) to talk about some of your fears and frustrations in dealing with depressed people.

15) Some people live with depression for a lifetime and go through regular bouts of lows. They make family and other caregivers weary of caring under pressure—a weariness that professionals have called "compassion fatigue." Caring for hurting people can be incredibly exhausting. Take note of family members who are worn down from helping a depressed family member. They need help and a break from the pressure as well.

16) Depressed people usually suffer from a chemical imbalance that can be corrected with medication. Doctors and psychiatrists may be able to offer certain anti-depressants that allow depressed individuals to live reasonably normal lives without difficult side effects. Medicated people need a regular evaluation of their medication and should consult their doctor as recommended.

17) Depressed people also need some form of counseling. Psychiatrists rarely do counseling; they primarily evaluate the effectiveness of medication with each patient. Ask if the parishioner is consulting with their doctor and is in some form of counseling care, especially if depression recurs. Ask permission to tell the pastor what you know.

For further reading:

Roy W. Fairchild, *Finding Hope Again: A Pastor's Guide to Counseling Depressed Persons* (San Francisco: 1980).

David Karp, *Speaking of Sadness* (Oxford: Oxford University Press, 1996).

Grace Ketterman, *Surviving the Darkness* (Nashville: Thomas Nelson, 1993).

Demitri Papolos and Janice Papolos, *Overcoming Depression* (New York: HarperPerennial, 1992).

Martin E. P. Seligman, *What You Can Change & What You Can't* (New York: Alfred A. Knopf, 1994).

Divorce

1) People with marital troubles don't usually ask for help until the relationship has almost deteriorated to the point of no repair. Nearly half of American marriages end in divorce, and one in three children lives in a broken home.

2) Our studies of divorcing couples indicate that a marriage can dissolve in seven phases of difficulty: private differences, intensified tension (under same roof but separate quarters), the involvement of a third party (friend or confidant), a stage of public awareness (open hostility), physical separation (two households), formal legal action, and the stage following a completed divorce status.

3) Victims of divorce are experiencing a stunning grief process stemming from the death of a relationship (see **Grief**). People who call you to report this difficulty express great trust in you, for it is not an easy experience to share with anyone.

4) When a marriage partner in conflict calls you for help, try to clarify what they want from you. Remember that we can't mend marriages or people; we can only provide support and help for those who want to work on their relationships.

5) Someone may call you mainly to vent feelings and share sorrow. They may ask you to intercede on their behalf with their spouse. Avoid getting involved in a "crossfire" where you become a third party asked to referee or judge between two frustrated marital partners.

6) Ask the marriage partner who called you if they have shared the problem with anyone else. Confidentiality and privacy are critical in marital struggles, because rumors and inaccurate stories can ruin reputations. Don't share anything you hear with anyone else except a pastor or counselor—with the person's permission.

7) One of the most difficult issues in marriage relationships is trust. When either partner feels betrayed, the recovery of faith in the other is a challenge. Thus, you must be careful as a listener trusted with personal information about a marital partnership from only one of the partners in the covenant.

8) Ask the person who called you if they have tried getting professional help for their trouble, or if both spouses would agree to go for help to a private and confidential source of care. If one of the partners is willing to go for counseling care, help them find options for counseling. A marriage can be helped even if only one of the partners is willing to get assistance.

9) Find out about the children in the family. Most distressed couples are so preoccupied with their own stress that they neglect their children, who are already dealing with the tension in the relationship. Are the children getting care, explanations, and help? Many adults don't realize how much pain and stress children absorb.

10) Assist a family in getting help even if the couple plan to separate or divorce. These families experience enough grief without having to face poor separation behaviors and unnecessary destructive actions. Counseling by pastors, pastoral counselors, or therapists can minimize further emotional harm. Encourage separating partners to get help for the process of disengagement.

11) Also encourage parishioners to continue counseling to work through the grieving process, which may take more than a year. Many divorcing partners experience relief and peace of mind in the first weeks of separation, especially if the marriage was stressful. They are

discouraged, however, when their delayed grief subjects them to bouts of anger, loneliness, depression, guilt, and low self-esteem (see **Anger**, **Depression**, and **Grief**). After all, the discontinued or modified relationship with a marital partner was an emotional investment of years.

For further reading:

Anita Brock, *Divorce Recovery* (Fort Worth TX: Worthy Publishing, 1988).

Bruce Fisher & Robert Alberti, *Rebuilding: When Your Relationship Ends* (Atascadero CA: Impact Publishers, 2000).

William J. Lederer and Don D. Jackson, *The Mirages of Marriage* (New York: W. W. Norton & Co., 1968).

Karen Keyser, *When Love Dies* (New York: The Guilford Press, 1993).

Judith Wallerstein & Joan Kelly, *Surviving the Breakup: How Children and Parents Cope with Divorce* (New York: Basic Books, 1979).

Children and Divorce

Children who live with divorcing parents need special attention, and if you are called to care for children of divorce, consider the following suggestions.

1) Children express grief quite differently from adults. They are less verbal, internalize feelings, and postpone dealing with feelings they don't recognize. Adults sometimes handle grief in these ways, but their grief is often more visible. When we fail to see grief signs in children that we recognize in adults, we often conclude either that the children are not grieving or that their hurt is minimal (see **Anger** and **Grief**).

2) Young children's entire sense of security and stability is shaken by divorcing parents. They will tend to show their pain physically at first—stomachaches, headaches, bed-wetting, clinging, increased crying, changes in eating habits, sleep problems, etc. This can escalate into a gradual withdrawal and light depression.

3) Predictable schedules help children find stability during the stress of divorce. As much as possible, recommend to parting parents that they

work hard at establishing a routine that children can count on during this time of upheaval.

4) With the parents' permission, share the family situation with trusted church members who see the child regularly. Encourage the parents to do the same with caregivers and teachers who work with the child.

5) One way children share their feelings and process their pain is by telling stories or completing stories we give them. They also use play as a way of dealing with their distress and respond best to a caregiver they know well. Encourage parents to find adults with whom children feel free to share their concerns.

6) Help divorcing adults watch for other signs of trouble. Children often assume responsibility for the divorce (especially young children), and need to be reassured by the parents that they are not responsible for the marriage or its breakup. Children in a family also fight with each other when stressed over the family problem. They tend to displace their pain and anger onto a brother or sister when they are actually angry at their parents for "dissolving" the family.

7) Children and young people also struggle to find God in the process of the family breakup. Younger children have trouble expressing how they feel about God. God (like their parents) is one of the remaining forces they must still count on for their own survival. Help children know that God won't abandon them, since they may feel that their parents have. Help them also know that it is okay to be confused about what God is doing in all their pain and loss.

8) Support groups are available to help teenagers and older children of divorce deal with their often delayed grief. Specific groups like ACD (Adult Children of Divorce) meet in churches and other charitable organizations in many communities. If no such group exists, ask your church leadership to help start one; several churches can work together to offer this ministry. Schools also have resources, and community

agencies often provide support groups for those who have experienced loss.

9) Remember that divorce is a grief experience even for those who are restructuring a new family; it is the death of a family that has lived together for years. Help family members not to confuse relief with recovery. Recovery takes a great deal of time.

For further reading:

Michaelene Mundy, *Sad Isn't Bad* (Caring One Series for Children) (Saint Meinrad IN: Abbey Press, 1999).

David Elkind, *The Hurried Child* (Reading MA: Addison-Wesley Publishing, 1981).

M. Ford, A. Ford, and S. Ford, *My Parents Are Divorced, Too* (Washington, D.C.: Magination Press, 1997).

Kenneth F. Parker & Van Jones, *Every Other Weekend* (Nashville: Thomas Nelson Publishers, 1993).

Edward Teyber, *Helping Children Cope with Divorce* (San Francisco: Jossey-Bass, 1992).

Grief

People experience many kinds of loss during a lifetime, and losses of great significance intensify the grief experience. Earlier we described caregiving for dying people processing their own death (**Death and Dying**). Here we offer insight into the grief experienced by people who lose a loved one through death. Grief is also a response to other losses: a job change, a broken relationship, a divorce, a geographical relocation, a pregnancy loss, a change in status, the development of a handicap, chronic illness, aging, the loss of a dream, etc.

1) When grief occurs people go through a set of experiences for an extended period of time. Each of us responds differently to loss, and the families in which we grew up (families of origin) are usually the most influential model for how we express our grief. Become a student of your parishioner's bereavement journey.

2) Sometimes we begin to experience a loss before it actually occurs. For example, the spouse of an Alzheimer's Disease patient may experience the loss of certain qualities of the person before the person actually passes away (anticipated grief). Some people move through different experiences and get "stuck" in the healing *process* (arrested grief) so that they don't move on toward full healing. For example, a person who is fired from their job may become so consumed with bitterness that they fail in the next place of employment.

3) Sometimes grief responses are delayed and only show up months later. People who assume the role of "rescuer" or "stabilizer" in a family

often postpone their grief in order to take care of everybody else in the family.

4) Grief reactions include (not necessarily in this order):

- *Shock:* The sudden impact or realization that someone/something valued has been taken or lost. The jolting effect of stunning news can produce shock. Shock is characterized by a glazed look; mechanical responses to questions; cold, "clammy" hands; and a stunned, temporary inability to respond to events—an "attention paralysis." Note what you see and hear; the survivor may not register much that is said and may need a few small decisions made for them until they can respond and focus.

- *Numbness:* Out-of-touch with feelings and a seemingly "flat" response to the news of a loss. Numbness is evident in little emotional expression and a withdrawn look that signifies a detachment sometimes considered "God's anesthesia," which allows the person to survive the intensity of the moment. A detached emotional reaction, sometimes misunderstood to reflect little feeling for a loss, actually provides a controlled way to survive overwhelming feelings so that the person can do what is required at the moment. Reassure those who are numb that the reaction is normal and that feelings will return.

- *Onset of Emotions:* A rush of feelings that breaks through the numbness with tears and emotional intensity. Sorrow and pain are evident, distress is heavy, and the reality of the loss is overwhelmingly apparent. Sobbing and emoting may be intense at some moments. The person may experience a release of numerous physical and emotional reactions to the loss, including shaking, convulsing, and recurring tears. It's best to say little at such times; acknowledge and affirm the importance of the person's feelings, and encourage their expression of these feelings.

- *Depression:* A mood swing to low point, loss of appetite, withdrawal and quiet sadness, lethargic reaction to events, and lack of interest in any activity. The person experiences deep sadness and feelings of disconnection with others; he or she often desires to be alone. A sense of helplessness and hopelessness can overwhelm a person. Provide a quiet presence, invite the person to tell you if they need to be alone or with others, and ask them to share thoughts and feelings if desired (see **Depression**).

- *Stabbing Memories:* Sudden and unpredictable recall of certain painful memories or recollections of the deceased (or of what was lost). The person may experience stunning flashbacks that evoke vivid memories and strong emotional impulses. These flashbacks are jarring, brief, but intensely sad remembrances. A time of peace of mind and calm may be interrupted by an unexpected connection that brings back an event or memory (a song, a gesture, a visual reminder, a color, an aroma, etc.). The most distressing part of this experience is that the griever may be in a public place sharing a pleasant moment, when they are suddenly stunned by the "stabbing" return of a memory that triggers a deep and powerful sadness. Help them know that their experience is normal, that it will not last forever, and that they have the right to seek privacy as they need it.

- *Bouts with Anger/Guilt:* Strong feelings of resentment and anger may eventually surface, and the bereaved person may suddenly face the injustice of the loss, its permanence, or its impact on the future. Anger is sometimes fueled by the fact that the person had no control over the event and was not given choices. Grieving people feel angry at others for not having lost as they have lost, and then they feel guilty for thinking such thoughts. They also feel guilty about their anger at a loved one for "abandoning" them, for not giving them an opportunity to say goodbye, or for having no chance to forgive and be forgiven for something. Grieving people also struggle with anger toward God for not controlling or for allowing the loss. Then, feeling guilty about these feelings toward God, they struggle with where God is when they are most in need. Bereaved people feel angry with

themselves, with others, with the deceased, and with God. They
need to be told that their anger is normal. Remind grieving believers
that their anger is an expression of their care, not something to feel
embarrassed or ashamed of (see **Anger** and **Guilt and Shame**).

• *Selective Memories:* Those who grieve sometimes recall distorted
memories of traits, conflicts, virtues, and behaviors of the deceased.
Perhaps only the good is remembered; sometimes only the bad. Love
and emotion can exaggerate memories and play tricks on the imagination. Caregivers help most in such moments by listening patiently
and helping the bereaved maintain appropriate perspective. This
phase of grieving often creates a temptation to idolize the deceased,
and a caregiver's contribution here is to affirm that the deceased was
loved, but still a human being. As a gift of care, listen to the sacred
memories.

• *Reestablishment of a Routine:* Survivors of a traumatic loss find security in returning to a routine that gives life predictable boundaries
and expectations. Encourage your grieving friend to return to a
schedule of work and responsibility as soon as feasible. Sadness and a
recurring depressive state will come and go; joy and laughter are rare
at first. The point of a routine is not that life automatically returns to
"normal," but that the individual normalizes their day and can count
on the security of a predictable daily pattern. This allows them to
continue the journey of recovery. Caregiver and survivor will both
notice that during these times the periods of sad moments grow
shorter, the tears occur less often and are briefer, and the survivor
becomes more active again.

• *Acceptance of the Loss and Moments of Joy:* Slowly but surely, the
person gradually accepts the reality of life past the loss, and the
return to a routine soon brings moments of joy, brief anticipation of
the future (instead of living entirely day to day), and fewer depressive
bouts. Laughter grows more spontaneous, flashes of hope appear,
and an increased release from preoccupation about the loss occurs.
The grieving person organizes their life apart from the loss.

Acknowledge and affirm the survivor's recognition of the reality of death and the need to "live on" themselves.

• *Recovery of Joy:* Caregivers notice in this phase of the survivor's recovery that depression and isolation are rare, the griever structures their life with a new sense of purpose and hope, and new goals are set. Sometimes called "resurrection," this movement is long in coming, but as important as any other experience in the movement toward "newness of life."

5) Keep in mind ways to help throughout the process of recovery from a loss. In the weeks following the funeral, after family and relatives have returned home and life assumes a routine, a note of comfort or a brief call by the caregiver to the mourner can make a world of difference. So many people expect survivors to "get over it and move on," as if such a shift were possible for human beings created in the image of God! The fact that we bond and belong (as God intends us to) means that the experience of loss is a deeply-felt grief that requires a long process of healing.

6) Listen periodically to the variety of feelings the griever has, without evaluating or judging their content. Acknowledge the person's right to hurt, to feel frustrated, angry, numb, bewildered, and listless. One of your greatest contributions after a loss is to listen with compassion to the anger, frustration, pain, and sorrow. These are the normal "steps" (rites of passage) through which a believer begins to accept the reality of loss and accepts the invitation gradually to reorganize life in a brand new way.

For further reading:
Kenneth J. Doka, *Living With Grief After Sudden Death* (New York: Taylor & Francis, 1994).

Kenneth J. Doka & Joyce D. Davidson, *Living With Grief* (Philadelphia: Brunner/Mazel, 1998).

Kenneth R. Mitchell & Herbert Anderson, *All Our Losses, All Our Griefs* (Philadelphia: Westminster Press, 1983).

Words/Actions to Avoid When Working with a Grieving Person

1) "It's for the best." (How do *you* know it's for the best?)

2) "It's all in God's plan." (How do *you* know what God wanted?)

3) "I'm glad she's no longer suffering." (Let the surviving loved one say this before you do.)

4) "It's time to get on with your life." "Move on." "Get over it."

5) Interruptions. Allow the grieving person to talk about their loss.

6) Reminders of the faults of the deceased person.

7) Unsolicited advice. Especially avoid advice on what or how the grieving person should feel.

8) Criticism or judgment. The person needs to be able to trust you to hear their grief with an open heart and mind.

9) Some people tend to avoid a grieving person because they aren't sure what to say. You can always *listen*.

Words to Avoid When a Child Dies

1) "At least you have your other children."

2) "At least you're young; you can try again."

3) "God must have needed a little angel up there."

4) "Let's not question God's wisdom."

5) "At least you didn't know the child." (stillbirth/miscarriage)

6) "Maybe the baby had something wrong with him. It's for the best."

7) "Please don't cry."

For further reading:

Judith R. Bernstein, *When the Bough Breaks: Forever After the Death of a Son or Daughter* (Kansas City: Andrew McMeel Publishing, 1997).

Mark Gellman & Thomas Hartman, *Lost & Found: A Kid's Book for Living Through Loss* (New York: Morrow Junior Books, 1999).

Richard S. Hipps, *When A Child Dies* (Macon GA: Smyth & Helwys, 1996).

Therese Huntley, *Helping Children Grieve* (Minneapolis: Augsburg Press, 1991).

Nancy Kohner & Alix Henley, *When a Baby Dies* (San Francisco: HarperCollins, 1995).

Alan Wolfelt, *Death and Grief: A Guide for Clergy and Others*, Accelerated Development, 1988.

Words for the Grieving Person

1) "I'm sorry." "I care." "I love you" (if you do).

2) "I'm here to listen." (Then talk little and listen attentively.)

3) "I can only imagine how difficult this time is for you."

4) "You've been strong and helpful for your family. I hope you know you don't have to be strong all the time. It's okay to let your feelings out sometimes."

5) "It's okay to be angry and frustrated—it's part of loving."

6) "It's okay to cry. I may cry with you."

7) Share your feelings of pain and loss for the deceased.

8) Tell the survivor positive things about their care and the value of the deceased.

9) Share happy memories as appropriate.

For further reading:
Emily Lane Waszak, *Grief: Difficult Times—Simple Steps* (Washington, D.C.: Accelerated Development, 1997).

Important Facts about Grief

1) Anger, rage, confusion, frustration, and fear are all natural responses to grief.

2) Grieving a loss takes time (more than a year). Everyone grieves differently.

3) Resist the temptation to avoid the bereaved or to avoid talking about the deceased.

4) Silence can be an important pause. Hesitate to break it.

5) Survivors of loss experience the pain of loss for a long time. Expect shifts in mood.

6) Loved ones always remember that "anniversaries" of events are important.

7) Invite a survivor to talk about their feelings, but don't force it.

Guilt and Shame

1) Sometimes a parishioner is overwhelmed by a profound, almost paralyzing feeling of guilt or shame. They may call us, desperate to find relief from the weight of an unresolved or unfinished issue.

2) How we respond to a troubled friend has much to do with whether they will feel accepted and helped by our conversation. Our willingness to listen attentively to their thoughts and feelings helps calm them and makes our job of discovering the problem easier.

3) People sometimes feel unforgiven for certain things they either did or failed to do. Because many of our faith traditions do not have a formal ritual for confession, many church members don't know what to do with their guilt and shame. Everyone needs a priest now and then.

4) Guilt can reach a crisis proportion if it distracts someone from their responsibilities or consumes a large amount of time. Guilt or shame can also lead to depression and rob people of precious energy and time that could be used for better purposes. From a Christian point of view, believers are not meant to spend so much time worrying about an "unforgiven" past that they are not free to live in the present.

5) People paralyzed by uncommon guilt or shame need professional care, and you can help by reminding them that nothing can separate them from the love of God in Christ Jesus—regardless of what they have done or failed to do (Romans 8:33-39).

6) Shame usually involves feelings of low self-worth and the anticipation of embarrassment or humiliation if someone were to find out (as with Adam and Eve in Genesis 3:6-10). In contrast to guilt, a response to something we did, shame is more concerned with who we are.

7) There are many different kinds of shame. Imagined shame is the created suspicion that we have some awful secret to hide that could be detected at any moment. If discovered, the secret will unmask us and ruin our reputation. Irrational shame is the humiliation of feeling constantly inferior, unacceptable, and unforgivable.

8) When someone chooses to share their feelings of shame or guilt, listen thoughtfully and with care to what they say. Help them identify the specific issue about which they feel shame or guilt. "What is it that you are ashamed of, John?" "Where do you think this guilt is coming from, Mary?" The clearer the parishioner can identify the source of their distress, the more manageable the problem will appear . . . and the smaller it may look. Remember, however, to invite the information but *never* coerce it.

9) If the guilt-ridden person seems to set aside your assurances that God can forgive anything, they likely need in-depth counseling care. Some people become obsessed with a sin or a thought to the point that they need professional care in order to break the vicious cycle of self-condemnation, which repeats painful memories over and over again without relief.

10) If you are a trusted listener and the parishioner is not controlled by unhealthy thought patterns, you may play a part in helping them reconcile with God and with themselves by doing three things: Listen to the thoughts and feelings of the person without judging them; ask them if they are sorry and repent of whatever deed or thought that troubles them; remind them that God has promised to forgive us and purify us of anything we confess (Psalm 32:5, 1 John 1:9, James 5:15-16).

11) Some people are so enmeshed in their guilt that they cannot accept forgiveness. They need pastoral counseling. Help them find relief and grace by connecting them with a therapist. Remember to keep in touch, so they don't feel rejected.

For further reading:

David Belgum, *Guilt: Where Religion and Psychology Meet* (Englewood Cliffs NJ: Prentice Hall, 1963).

Lewis B. Smedes, *Forgive and Forget: Healing the Hurts We Don't Deserve* (San Francisco: Harper & Row, 1984); idem, *Shame and Grace* (San Francisco: Harper & Row, 1993).

Homosexuality and Gender Identity

1) People struggling with personal identity issues sometimes experience a "homosexual panic." Homosexuality and gender identity confusion can cause a great deal of anxiety and concern. Because this issue often creates strong emotional reactions, it is important that a caregiver understands what the individual tells them.

2) If a family member calls expressing the fear that someone in their family is "gay," take time to listen carefully to what they say, and help them understand clear distinctions.

- "Effeminate" or "masculine" mannerisms have little to do with sexual identity, preference, or behaviors.
- People who prefer friendships with others of their own gender are not necessarily "gay" or confused.
- People who choose a single lifestyle over a married lifestyle mostly do so because of significant personal priorities, not sexual issues (note examples in the Bible: Elijah, Jesus, Paul, etc.).
- Affectionate people who express needs for physical and emotional intimacy are not necessarily seeking sexual intimacy.
- People who realize that their sexual attraction is toward people of the same gender don't choose that attraction; they discover it (and most of them fight the feelings throughout their lives).
- Most people who discover that they are attracted to people of the same gender never act on their feelings or become involved sexually with a same-sex partner.

- Adolescents and young adults struggle with a variety of feelings (and hormones) that they do not understand. They sometimes label these feelings "homosexual" by mistake.
- People who describe themselves as "homosexual" or "gay" are not necessarily either promiscuous or even sexually active at all.

3) If a parishioner has a "private matter" to discuss with you, they may desire to talk with you about their fears or anxieties concerning feelings or fantasies they have—including sexual feelings they don't understand. If you are comfortable responding to such an invitation, assure them of your care, confidentiality, and willingness to talk. *If you are not comfortable with this kind of conversation*, offer them suggestions of other people who can help them. Some people who struggle with homosexual fantasies become depressed or suicidal. Mention a pastor, a pastoral counselor, or a therapist you trust. Call the church office if you have no resources.

4) If you choose to listen, suggest a place with *appropriate* privacy (the church office, a conference room, a restaurant). The anxious parishioner needs your help in feeling safe about this conversation. Sometimes they can neither speak in a home, a church office, or a workplace but may feel protected in a public area that provides some degree of privacy. Avoid completely isolating yourselves in situations of great vulnerability.

5) As you listen, try not to make assumptions about what you know or don't know. Just because a parishioner says they have strange, shameful, or confusing feelings, don't assume that these are homosexual feelings. Just because the person describes sexual fantasies, don't assume they are sexually active. Just because the person uses the words "gay" or "homosexual," don't assume that they are accurately labeling their feelings. Finally, just because the person describes a homosexual encounter, don't assume that they are gay.

6) Help people make a distinction between *orientation* and *behavior* in sexual matters. Orientation refers to an attraction or identification, not an act or behavior. For example, if you describe yourself to

another person as a heterosexual, you have told them only what your identity or attraction is, not how sexually active or inactive you are. The same distinction applies to homosexual; it is not an act or behavior. Homosexuals constitute about four to twelve percent of the population in the United States and comprise about the same percentage of any church membership, though over ninety-two percent describe themselves as never having been sexually active. Some are even married heterosexually and have children.

7) When parishioners seek understanding and help with gender identiy issues, send them to people who can help them manage and control their sexual feelings and behavior, just the way you would advise anyone else. Christians struggling with homosexual feelings are no more likely to attempt to woo or seduce someone than a heterosexual believer, nor do they have any mysterious "power" to do so (a common myth).

8) Reassure people struggling with homosexual issues that they cannot "teach" or "transmit" homosexual feelings, just as a heterosexual cannot teach or transmit their heterosexual feelings.

9) Remind guilt-ridden parishioners who seem overwhelmed by condemnation and shame for their feelings that people struggling with gender identity and sexual thoughts, like any other person, need forgiveness for inappropriate or irresponsible sexual fantasies they have. *Everyone* needs forgiveness for sexual fantasies (John 8:7-9).

10) Condemnation and lecturing do little to help troubled people facing sexual struggles. The distraught parishioner may need to be reminded that they did not choose to have these feelings. Continued studies affirm that a "gay" sexual orientation is at best a combination of biology and extremely early environment—first or second year of life—and not a preference that individuals seek or consciously choose.

11) Many folks facing these difficult sexual feelings are fearful of being discovered for who they are and being rejected by their family and

loved ones, including their church. Help them deal with the anxiety of this issue in a safe environment by sharing their struggle (with their permission!) only with people who can maintain confidentiality.

12) If a person confirming their homosexual orientation wants to share this burden (and it is a burden, not a blessing) with their family, help them rehearse how to do it, or help them find a counselor who can assist them with this delicate conversation. Remember that parents of homosexual children often feel guilty and responsible, and they usually respond first with grief and anger.

13) Unless you are a skilled counselor, avoid delving into the parishioner's choices about whether or not they will become sexually active, or how they will share their orientation with the church. Most congregations need a great deal of preparation and education before they can begin to understand the difference between orientation and behavior, the fact that gay people don't choose their orientation, that their congregation already has (and has always had) bisexual and homosexual members, or that a homosexual person does not need a special repentance/conversion from which heterosexuals are exempt.

14) Help your congregation and its leadership discuss this complex issue in an atmosphere of biblical assumptions so they may gain understanding, balance grace with responsibility, respect differences in a Christ-like way, and determine what boundaries they believe are in keeping with Christ's way and will. Never undertake an educational issue such as this in conjunction with an individual's request to have the church "act" on the homosexual person's situation or role. Delicate issues should always be separated from personalities for the sake of fair discussions.

15) Make sure that you examine your own feelings and prejudices about this issue as you attempt to help someone challenged with it. Your feelings (and values) will become clear to the parishioner.

For further reading:

Bruce Hilton, *Can Homophobia Be Cured?* (Nashville: Abingdon Press, 1992).

James B. Nelson & Sandra P. Longfellow, *Sexuality and the Sacred* (Louisville: Westminter/John Knox Press, 1994).

Letha Scanzoni & Virginia Ramey Mollenkott, *Is the Homosexual My Neighbor?* (New York: Harper & Row, 1978).

Illness

Hospitalization and Emotional Illness

1) When a family member calls for help, your calm response and direction will reduce their anxiety.

2) If they report signs of emotional distress, ask if other family members (or anyone else familiar with the person) have mentioned or noticed unusual behavior/demeanor.

3) Ask: Is anyone in immediate danger? Is someone's safety at issue? Are medication, transportation, and possible weapons under control?

4) Ask them what other steps they may have already taken. Has a family physician been consulted? Other professionals? Has anyone recommended hospitalization?

5) Is it appropriate or helpful for you to join the family—or meet them at an institution? Do they know where to go? Do they have transportation? Do they know directions to the facility? Do they have a family/friend with them?

6) What calls can you make for them? Has the pastor been called? They might name (or you might suggest) essential family members, doctors, friends for immediate support, deacons, hospitals, church office for control/distribution of information, etc.

7) If the distressed person will not cooperate and needs hospitalization, either a family member or friend may be needed to help provide safe transportation and give the family moral support during admission. Emergency Medical Service or the local police force are better options if the person shows signs of getting out of control or causing harm.

8) Interpret to patient and family the value of medication as a temporary stabilizer, especially for heavy depression, rest, perspective, and family care. Just as with a physical illness, emotional illness sometimes needs to be treated with medication.

9) Shorter, more frequent contact with family and brief, supportive care contact with the hospitalized person (after medical/patient clearance) is the best approach to visitation. Take note of restricted visitation hours/days and the allowed length of visit. Sometimes a phone call to the patient is most beneficial.

10) Explain to family the nature of the emotional issue only if you know what is involved. Assist them in gaining clarity and peace of mind by learning what questions they want to ask the medical and psychiatric personnel.

11) Involve the congregation only after consultation with the family (and the pastor) so that trusted church members can be of practical help. The family needs emotional support to deal with the shock of hospitalization.

12) Remind the family that emotional illness is nothing to be embarrassed about, and help them rehearse an explanation or comment to friends and neighbors who may call to help. They might even create a list of what friends can do to assist them right now.

REMEMBER:
- Hospitalization interrupts family stability and patient independence.
- Financial costs (loss of income, hospitalization) are major stress issues.
- Institutionalization can weaken persons and contribute to discouragement.
- Length of illness and clarity of diagnosis affect family hope.
- Interpretation of God's care in mental illness is crucial.
- Awkwardness and embarrassment are family issues.
- Fear, hesitation, and initiative are faith community issues.
- Home reentry moments are as challenging as hospital admission time.

Hospitalization and Physical Illness

1) If you plan to visit someone, always call the hospital first. Hospital schedules (x-rays, tests), meals, dismissal, etc., change from day to day, and you can save time by visiting when patients are available.

2) Call the church office, indicate your plan to visit, and coordinate with the ministers so that visits are scheduled in brief increments and don't tire or overwhelm the patient.

3) If possible, stop at a nurse's station to assure that it is acceptable to walk into the patient's hospital room. Nurses can help us avoid awkward entries during baths, examinations, changing clothes, etc. If patient is asleep, ask if it is appropriate to wake them, or leave a note. How much company have they had?

4) Make visits brief; patients tell us that ten to fifteen minutes are best. Ask the patient if this is a good moment to come in, and be aware that right after surgery patients are either heavily sedated (and therefore will not remember much) or in great discomfort and need only a short visit or no visit at all.

5) Avoid spending much time talking about yourself; you are there to focus on the patient. Spend your time on the issues at hand. Are they concerned about medical news they have just received? Are they waiting for information (has a doctor or nurse been by)? Avoid "small talk," the superficial conversations about weather, sports, and other distracting nonessentials. Simply ask them how they are doing.

6) Avoid describing someone else's "similar" problem, unless it's a brief comment that encourages them. People don't need to hear gory stories about someone else's struggle with the same disease. They are aleady anxious.

7) Don't say, "I know just how you feel" or "I understand" unless you really do. Such words will otherwise sound false. Be honest. Say, "I can't begin to imagine your discomfort, but I hope you know that I care."

8) Respond to feelings by recognizing them. Don't avoid them or try to argue them away. If someone is angry at God, let them express that anger. God does not need our protection; God has survived many a psalmist's anger. Receive the anger, and acknowledge the feelings behind it. "I can tell that you are very upset and frustrated with what is happening. Please know that God understands your anger and pain."

9) If you know a church member is in the hospital, always make sure the church office knows as well. Don't assume someone else gave them the information.

10) Avoid touching the bed when you visit someone in the hospital. Any jarring movement can disturb or cause pain. If possible, stand next to the bed in a position that makes it easier for the patient to see your face without straining to look up at you. It will also help if you leave after a short visit. Understand that if five friends come by that day and each stays thirty minutes, a sick person is subjected to two and a half hours of constant conversation in one day.

11) If you are comfortable voicing a prayer, ask the person if there is anything they would like for you to pray about. They may mention their greatest anxiety, so make sure you pay attention. Don't pray too long. Focus on the need, remember what has happened and what will soon happen, and be conscious of the patient's separation from their family.

12) Remember that "minor" surgery is only minor if you are not having it yourself. As you leave, ask, "Is there anything I can do for you before I go?"

13) If you visit on certain schedules, tell the person when you will come again. If family is visiting, include them in the conversation, but make sure you focus on the patient's care and health. If the family needs to visit, be brief, excuse yourself, and come back at a later time. (Richard K. Young, *The Pastor's Hospital Ministry* [Nashville: Broadman, 1954].)

Homebound Patient

People who are home ill (or who return ill from the hospital) need care. If you are called to visit the ill in their home, consider the following suggestions.

1) Always call before you visit. Even in rural and informal settings, there are too many unpleasant surprises and awkward possibilities for the family and the caregiver. For example, you may find someone so ill that they need no visitors; you may come during a mealtime; you may find the person sleeping, not needing to be disturbed; or you may find only one person at home, creating a delicate situation if they are of the opposite gender.

2) Calling ahead is also good use of your time, because you can avoid an unnecessary trip. If calling on the telephone is not an option, always respect the family's privacy by asking questions like these before you enter the home: "Is this a good time to visit?" "Would you rather

I come by another time?" "When is the best time for visitors?" Sometimes a quick visit at the door provides all the information you need for rescheduling, and your mere presence communicates your interest in the parishioner.

3) Only carry flowers if you know the parishioner has no breathing problems. Only carry food if you know ahead of time that it will be appreciated. Only stay longer than fifteen minutes if the patient is anxious and truly desires to talk longer about a concern.

4) Make sure that you position yourself in a way that makes it easy for a bedridden person to see and talk with you. Avoid getting close to the bed or jarring a recovering surgery patient.

5) Offer to shake hands or touch only after you know that it will neither hurt nor bother the patient. Be aware of sore arms from IVs (intravenous feeding/medication tubes).

6) If a patient whispers, they may have a sore throat from tubes placed in the mouth during procedures. Be considerate and don't overwhelm them with questions they feel obligated to answer.

7) If a sick parishioner invites you to stay longer when you prepare to leave, consider it a gesture of kindness on their part, but don't linger. Sick or recovering patients often don't realize how tiring a visit is until it ends.

8) If you are comfortable doing so, offer to pray as you conclude your visit. Focus on the patient's needs, avoid long prayers and "empty phrases" (Matthew 6:5-7), and ask the parishioner if there is anything they would like for you to pray about.

9) Before you leave, ask if there is anything you can do for them—an errand, a message, a favor, a call, etc.

10) Make sure someone at the church office knows that you visited and knows what you learned about the patient's needs and preferences. This information will help them schedule other visits.

For further reading:
Kenneth J. Doka, *Living with Grief: When Illness Is Prolonged* (New York: Taylor & Francis, 1996).

Marlene E. Hunter, *Making Peace with Chronic Pain* (New York: Brunner/Mazel Publishers, 1996).

Terminally Ill Patient

1) Sometimes a parishioner is released to their home because they are expected to die soon, and they and their family have chosen to spend this time together in the most comfortable way possible. Palliative care involves giving medication to a dying patient that will ease their pain and suffering.

2) The dying patient faces several major issues: losing control of their health, grieving their upcoming death (see **Death and Dying**), reviewing their life, planning the disposition of their property (and often planning their own funeral), processing their family members' grief over their impending death, discussing spiritual issues, and managing their own anxieties and fears.

3) There are several stages in terminal illness, and your visit may occur during any of them:

• suspected life-threatening condition (but not confirmed);
• a declared medically irreversible condition, in which parishioner and family face the reality of approaching death;
• active and accelerated end of life experiences, which often occur the last six months of life; hospice care becomes available at this time.

4) Sometimes the family wants privacy and rest; sometimes they want company. Sometimes the parishioner is so exhausted that they may

only visit for a short time. Be flexible. Follow their needs and schedules when you call.

5) The parishioner and the family may wish to talk about spiritual
issues with you. "Where is God in human suffering? Did God cause
this illness? Am I being punished? Why are our prayers not answered?"
Respond mostly by listening, and don't feel responsible to answer
questions for which you have no answers. If you feel inadequate to
deal with some of these questions, suggest to the patient that they discuss them with their pastor, the hospice chaplain, or a pastoral
counselor.

6) Be aware that the patient probably is (or soon will be) willing to
talk about their own death. They are often ready to talk about death
before their family members are ready. Some people erroneously
believe that if they participate in conversations about death, then their
dying family member will "give up hope." Help them realize that hope
and faith have little to do with a patient's need to process their own
feelings. It is helpful to everyone involved when they allow their dying
family member to talk about dying.

7) Don't force anyone to talk about death or dying; however, encourage and allow the conversations. Take note that in order for you to
enter such dialogue with the patient, you must come to terms with
your own feelings about dying and death. Your awkward feelings or
anxieties will surface in your conversations with the dying parishioner.

8) When you face a question or an issue that is difficult for you to
manage, admit that you don't know the answer and simply promise to
find out. You might have someone who does know the answer visit
with the parishioner. Honesty is essential in the care of dying people.

For further reading:

George Lee Harper Jr., *Living with Dying* (Grand Rapids MI: Eerdmans Publishing, 1992).

Rob George & Peter Houghton, *Healthy Dying* (London: J. Kingsley Publishers, 1997).

George S. Lair, *Counseling the Terminally Ill* (New York: Taylor & Francis, 1996).

Rosalie Peck & Charlotte Stephanics, *Learning to Say Goodbye* (Bristol PA: Accelerated Development, 1987).

Imprisonment

1) When a family member is arrested or detained, the resulting anxiety affects the entire family. If you hear that someone has been arrested or is serving time in jail, take initiative toward that family by calling or writing a note that indicates your awareness and care.

2) Families who deal with incarceration often feel embarrassed to mention the situation. They need care and support but aren't sure how to ask for it. You "break the ice" when you call and let them know that you are willing to talk with them and support them.

3) When you call, ask the family what you can do to help. Find out accurate details about the current situation. Sometimes rumors spread false information, and one of your contributions may be to control them. Get the facts, but don't press anyone to say more than they wish to say.

4) Some families are intensely private about family crises and prefer to handle their emergencies on their own. If such is the case, you may prefer to write the family a note, indicating that your prayers and interest are with them and that you are glad to support them in any way.

5) People arrested for misdemeanors (minor offenses) are usually not detained more than a day or two and may be released "on bail," money paid by the family and held at a government facility to guarantee that the person detained will appear in court for a hearing or trial and not simply disappear. Common misdemeanor charges are driving

under the influence of alcohol (DUI), shoplifling, or writing a check without sufficient funds to cover the expense (WSF).

6) A felony is legally a more serious offense and often requires a larger bail amount, an extended arrest while waiting on a hearing, or incarceration until a court procedure takes place. In either case, both the detained person and the family experience a significant amount of stress.

7) Support for a the family after an arrest and before a trial consists mostly of notes of encouragement, telephone calls, brief visits to family (when appropriate), and inquiries to assure that legal and spiritual assistance is being offered.

8) Families and their accused relatives face a great deal of anxiety when they go to court for a hearing, where a judge presides over a potential case and determines if it is to be dismissed, acted upon, or sent to trial. They also experience trauma when they must appear in court for any procedure, so if you are close enough to the family, you may ask them if you can go to court with them and serve as a silent presence and support.

9) Before you plan a visit to the county or city jail, ask family and authorities if, where, and when it is appropriate for family, lawyers, and clergy to visit. Write the incarcerated person a brief letter until a visit is appropriate.

10) There is a dramatic difference between an arrest and full-term imprisonment. People who are arrested usually await a court procedure that determines if they will "serve time" (actually spend time in jail after a particular sentence). When a sentence of time in prison has been decided—and the length of time depends on the severity of the crime—a person is sent from a county or city jail to a state or federal prison (penitentiary) to serve their time.

11) Support for a family and individual during incarceration consists of regular contact with the family and inmate. Calls and notes act as reminders that none of them are forgotten during their difficult time. When possible, visits are also encouraging. Remember that state and federal prisons make separation more difficult, since the family and the imprisoned person are rarely close geographically.

12) Families struggling with an arrested family member usually face financial challenges. Arrested people can lose their jobs and source of income, and they may require emergency funds in order to produce bail money. Legal fees, even for a hearing, involve an immediate outlay of funds. Family members left without one of the breadwinners struggle with meeting financial deadlines. Also, a family visiting an inmate at a distant state prison can spend a sizable amount of money in transportation, lodging, and food costs. Does your church have an emergency fund for people facing such challenges?

13) Remember to pray regularly for incarcerated parishioners and their families and to keep in touch with them. The absence of a family member in a home is a traumatic event, including the involuntary adjustment (for a family with children) of becoming a one-parent family for a period of time.

14) Church members can provide childcare for an adult who wishes to visit a spouse during imprisonment, and thus also assist in the preservation of a marital relationship. Incarceration is an enemy to marriage covenants! A few visits from friends during the imprisonment can make the difference between complete discouragement and rehabilitation in jail. Remember Christ's words in Matthew 25:36b: "I was in prison and you visited me."

15) Help other church members realize that asking questions about the family's welfare and the inmate's condition express love and care to the family, not discomfort. Encourage friends to ask the family questions like these. "How are you doing this week, Mary?" "What do you hear from John, and how is he managing?" "When do you think you

can visit him, and how can we help make that possible?" "Is there a better time for us to visit Jean? We think of her often and want to do what we can during this time of separation." "How are the kids doing, Lois?"

16) Remember these tips if you decide to visit someone in prison. Be prepared to be searched if you visit a parishioner in jail or in prison. These searches can seem invasive and personal, but are necessary for security. Arrange with an officer or attendant for the proper delivery of clothes, cash, cigarettes, candy, or any gifts you bring, remembering that in some places such gifts are prohibited. Never give an inmate cash directly. They have no safe way of storing money and can be robbed. Instead, talk with an officer about procedures for placing money in the inmate's account. Plan for a brief visit (10-15 minutes); say what you came to say early in the conversation in case you're given little time.

17) Expect that any mail you send will be screened or read before the parishioner receives it. Books or other materials may be denied for use by the inmate, unless the inmate has specifically requested them in writing.

18) Parishioners who have never been in jail before are usually scared and even traumatized by the event. Some judges use the shock of arrest or incarceration as a "wake-up call" to young offenders in hopes of stunning them into realizing what their futures may hold if they don't change behaviors. Listen to inmates patiently and caringly, and offer them as much consolation as you can.

19) Examine your own beliefs and prejudices before you visit an imprisoned parishioner. They are already anxious and worried; giving advice, lecturing, scolding, or judging them is of little value. They have likely heard all the condemnation they can take. Remind them with your presence and manner that they are not forgotten or cut off, that God is with them even when they feel alone, and that you care regardless. Avoid arguing with them, especially over whether they are

guilty or innocent. Let a lawyer handle the legal issues. Simply care for the imprisoned person.

20) People who have been given a sentence usually have an opportunity for early release based upon their behavior. A group of selected citizens called a parole board usually reviews an inmate's record and prison file several months before the full sentence is served. In most states the laws determine the timetable (a one-year sentence, for example, often means that a prisoner's file will be reviewed in four months; a two-year sentence is reviewed at six to eight months). If you hear your parishioner talk about going to the parole board, their time and behavior is being reviewed and they could possibly be released early (especially first-time offenders).

21) If you choose to visit a penal institution as a ministry to people you have not met, spend time acquainting yourself with prison procedures and with the behaviors of "repeat offenders." Some people have learned to survive most of their lives by deceiving people and ignoring laws, and you need to learn cautious ways to care for them.

For further reading:
Steve Gravett, *Coping with Prison* (New York; Cassell & Covington, 1999).
Gary R. Collins, ed., *Counseling for Family Violence & Abuse* (Waco TX: Word Books, 1987).

Jail and a Juvenile

1) Sometimes young people get in trouble with the law over a variety of behaviors. Minors, children up to eighteen years of age, are held and treated as juveniles by most state and federal officials. They face hearings and court appearances with their parents or guardians.

2) When youth are arrested for a misdemeanor or felony, juvenile court judges and other officials evaluate the severity of the offense in deciding whether or not to release them to the custody of their supervising adults.

3) A good number of youth today experiment with a variety of illegal drugs. They face arrest under a charge called "possession of a controlled substance." If they try to sell drugs, the more serious charge of "sale of a controlled substance" can be served.

4) Other frequent legal issues for juveniles involve the use of an alcoholic beverage while driving a car, shoplifting or theft, and running away from home. When a minor is charged with an offense, they usually must appear in court for a hearing or judgment. If they are not sent to jail for the infraction, they could be on probation under the supervision of a juvenile probation officer to whom they must periodically report (usually weekly).

5) Families with juveniles in legal trouble obviously struggle with stress. Whether they want support or not, it is appropriate for a Christian caregiver to indicate interest and support for the family and the youth.

6) Families facing legal issues with their children need pastoral counseling or another form of counseling that can assist them with behavior modification and impulse control. These exercises help people struggling with setting boundaries for themselves, especially with postponing gratification. There are also therapy groups for adolescents who have difficulty controlling inappropriate behavior or setting boundaries.

7) Encourage parents to participate in counseling sessions with their youth. Many young people develop poor behavior controls that have been modeled by the adults in their family.

8) If your church has a youth minister, or a Christian adult whom the youth respect, involve the person in caregiving with the young parishioner. When a church youth group is mature, its members can also serve as a safe "family" with whom the adolescent can grow and heal emotionally and spiritually.

9) Whatever you do, don't give up on the young person. Adolescents need space in order to assert their own personal identities. They often cannot put into words what they feel, but they know and respect honest, sincere, and humble caregivers.

For further reading:
Charles Shelton, *Pastoral Counseling with Adolescents and Young Adults* (New York: Crossroads, 1994).

Infertility/ Miscarriage

1) *Infertility* means the inability of a woman to achieve a pregnancy or carry a child to birth, or the inability of a man to create a pregnancy with his spouse. People who deal with this challenge experience frustration, depression, tension in their marriage, and a great amount of stress.

2) When a couple or individual, married but without children over a period of years, confide in you about stress in their marriage, one possible factor of the tension may be the trauma of infertility.

3) The gradual awareness by a couple that they may be unable to conceive a child can occasion significant grief. People facing the possibility of never having their own children biologically often confront the death of a dream, and even more, the death of who they planned to be (identity loss). In either case, such people need pastoral attention and spiritual care.

4) The involuntary loss of a fetus is also a traumatic grief crisis (see **Death and Dying** and **Grief**). One out of three expectant couples in this country experience a pregnancy loss. While many of their friends remain unaware that they were even expecting, the couple who suffers a miscarriage often must process the death of an unborn child and the possible death of their hopes and plans as a family.

5) Many expectant couples have waited years to have their own child, and their hopes and dreams are encouraged by the confirmation of

pregnancy. The sudden reversal of that positive news is difficult to absorb and even more difficult to share with others.

6) People who grieve the loss of a pregnancy are reluctant to talk about their loss because they feel foolish for grieving a miscarriage. They may also feel that the loss is a personal reflection of their inadequacy. You may help by reminding them that mothers often report feeling as emotionally and spiritually connected to an unborn child as they feel to children already born.

7) The common feelings of inadequacy and inferiority experienced by infertile couples are heightened in our society, which blesses parenting and often reduces couples without children to the position of a "second-class" citizen.

8) Help your families who face infertility by:

• encouraging couples to seek medical advice and pastoral counseling;
• offering/sponsoring a support group in your church or community for couples waiting to become pregnant (a national support system known as "Resolve" seeks to aid couples dealing with infertility and miscarriage);
• holding workshops or programs that educate and equip your church to minister to people during these crises.

9) If nothing else, encourage individuals or couples to attend counseling sessions, because those struggling to have a baby experience private tension and heightened stress.

10) When people resist counseling, accompany them to a support group. Sometimes one visit to a support group helps them realize how many people struggle with this issue, and how helpful it is to identify the enormous amounts of stress generated by the challenge of infertility.

11) Because many families and church communities are silent about miscarriage, few people realize the frequency with which they occur or the significance of losing an unborn baby. The physical impact of losing a fetus is the equivalent of major surgery, and the emotional and spiritual impact is enormous. Remind families of the importance of having regular medical consultations during infertility and miscarriage.

12) People who experience miscarriages have an additional need. They have the right to process their experience through a ceremony or ritual that helps them confront their loss and begin to heal. Some pastors are sensitive enough to suggest or recommend a private memorial service for the couple and perhaps family members they wish to invite. Talk to the couple about such an option. Many hospitals dispose of miscarriage remains routinely, and the couple has no opportunity to evaluate their options for a burial.

13) If infertility is confirmed and the couple chooses to consider adoption, assure that they are under the care of physicians, pastors, and other competent counselors. Some couples conclude that they cannot bear children biologically before receiving proper evaluation by a physician. In addition, adoption as an option is usually an even more stressful decision and needs careful and prayerful evaluation.

14) A large number of couples who choose to adopt later discover that they can have children biologically. Often the challenge for such families is managing the stress of having several children at once, and sometimes they struggle with caring for an adopted child as much as their biological child. Pastoral or private counseling should be encouraged, and the church caregiver may be the most trusted outsider who can recommend such care.

15) When you offer care by listening to the frustration and sorrow of those who struggle with infertility, remind them of the host of people in the Bible who suffered the same challenge.

For further reading:

Ellen Sarasohn Glazer, *Experiencing Infertility* (San Francisco: Jossey-Bass, 1995).

Michael R. Berma, *Hygeia: An Online Journal for Pregnancy and Neonatal Loss*, 1997, <http://hygeia.org/htm>.

Kim Kluger-Bell, *Unspeakable Losses* (New York: W. W. Norton, 1998).

Nelson & Ellen Kraybill, *Miscarriage: A Quiet Grief* (Scottsdale PA: Herald Press, 1990).

Thomas Moe, *Pastoral Care in Pregnancy Loss: A Ministry Long Needed* (New York: The Haworth Press, 1997).

Maureen Rank, *Free to Grieve* (Minneapolis: Bethany House, 1985).

Job Loss

1) People who lose a job face a series of difficulties. Caring for them during the crises that follow is important. Whether fired, laid off, or reassigned, the unemployed parishioner contends with loss of income, loss of dignity, and loss of identity.

2) If you know a church member who has lost a job, take initiative in friendship to ask how they are doing and how you can help. Although some people feel awkward at first describing themselves as "unemployed," almost everyone will appreciate your word of encouragement and interest.

3) If a church member calls to tell you that they have lost their job, consider it an invitation to ask them a few questions and offer your support. Some unemployed people feel embarrassed to say they are without work; perhaps they feel inadequate or unneeded if dismissed by an employer.

4) People who have lost a job often become depressed. Their depression stems from the grief of losing a position and from the steady negative comments they make to themselves concerning the situation. "I guess I was laid off because I was not a good employee." "If they thought what I was doing was important, I probably wouldn't have been dismissed." "Everyone else must have been doing a good job except me." "I really must not do anything right." "What am I going to do now? I bet I can't get a job after this." Caregiving involves helping a person recognize how their negative thinking contributes to their deep discouragement.

5) With the unemployed person's permission, discover how you can assist the transition from disengagement to reemployment. Some people need time to reassess their vocational hopes, and they use the job interruption as an opportunity to reflect and perhaps train for a new kind of work. Pray for patience and insight for them while they wait, and for creative imagination as they consider their skills, desires, and possibilities for the next job.

6) Some dismissed people have worked hard and need the break that the layoff or termination allows. They want a job, but they also need time for rest. Encourage those who are tired to rest and to review their life goals as they begin to look ahead.

7) Sometimes people who have been fired learn to distrust employers and job offers. They need a trusted friend who will slowly restore their confidence in other people and in themselves. If you can offer encouragement and confidence to an unemployed parishioner, you will help them build up their courage to begin again.

8) People who have been terminated often need two important things:

• they need to talk through their discouragement and low self-worth to avoid withdrawing and giving up on a new job;
• they need someone who believes in them to recommend them to potential employers and to offer leads and ideas on where to search for job opportunities.

9) Could you act as a reference for an unemployed parishioner? Does your church have a system for coordinating job opportunities that church members may be willing to offer the unemployed? Can your church (maybe in cooperation with other congregations) offer a "job fair" from time to time? What about a support group for people in transition from one employment to the next? You may be surprised to discover how many people leave a job, look for a job, and want to change jobs in a given year in your church community.

10) Remember the family of the fired or laid off member. They also struggle with concerns and fears and need to know that their church and its leadership care about them. A confidential "emergency fund" that keeps utilities paid and bills current during a family's search for employment can be a gift from God during anxious times.

11) Help the unemployed (who are grieving) reorganize their lives so that they can succeed again:

• Encourage them to accept the reality of the setback instead of not denying its occurrence.
• Invite them to find ways to express their feelings of frustration, loss, anger, and fear through regular contact with you or someone else.
• Help them find emotional support and spiritual care through family and friends they know.
• Assist them to structure a plan for finding a job, applying for jobs, and checking with helpful sources.
• Remind them to exercise regularly, eat well, and volunteer a few hours a week at their favorite charity. This will help them retain or recover a sense of worth.
• Alert them to resources and agencies where they may find opportunities and training for jobs they might desire.
• Suggest that they visit with a counselor who will help them understand that losing a job is a major grief experience that involves some loss of personal identity, but certainly not the end of all opportunities in life (see **Grief**).

12) Remember to pray for and with the unemployed in a helpful, not demeaning, way. Pray for God's guidance and perspective as they wait for the next job, for peace of mind in their anxieties and fears about the unknown, for courage in the waiting, for strength and peace of mind for their families, and for wisdom and insight as they seek a new job. Affirm their right to feel frustrated, cast aside, angry, and sometimes betrayed, but remind them that how they feel—and what the future will bring—are two entirely different things. Help them HOPE.

For further reading:

Bob Deits, *Life After Loss* (Tucson AZ: Fisher Books, 1992).

Parker J. Palmer, *Let Your Life Speak: Listening for the Voice of Vocation* (San Francisco: Jossey-Bass, 2000).

Mary Lynn Pulley, *Losing Your Job—Reclaiming Your Soul* (San Francisco: Jossey-Bass, 1997).

Mental Illness

1) If someone expresses concern that a friend or family member may be struggling with an emotional illness or breakdown, help them assess the situation by asking them to check for common signs of emotional disorder. Several of these signals together constitute need for serious inquiry or intervention. Following are common signs of severe emotional stress.

- Inappropriate or disproportionate reactions to events. Excessive reaction to an issue.
- Noticeable change in personality and/or behavior.
- Pronounced difference in eating/sleeping habits—too much or too little.
- Neglect of general appearance, dress, and grooming.
- Irritability, abusive or destructive demeanor/behavior.
- Irrational reasoning or judgment.
- Noticeable dysfunction in the discharge of responsibilities. Unable to perform normal activites. Difficulty with routine assignments.
- Preoccupation, distraction, withdrawal. Difficulty concentrating and focusing. Impaired memory.
- Dramatic mood swings; up one moment, down the next. Uncontrollable crying.
- Bizarre language. Words make no sense. Incoherent speech.
- Inability to perform routine daily functions (dressing, feeding self, etc.).
- Evidence of drug/artificial substance use and/or abuse.
- Uncharacteristc/altered behavior reported by family members.
- Intense depression.

2) If a cluster of these signs appears at one time, recommend to the family that they see the family doctor for a medical evaluation. The family doctor is the best avenue for a referral to a psychiatrist if needed.

3) If a family member is worried about the safety of the parishioner and needs a more urgent intervention, ask if the family member is able to transport the parishioner to a medical center emergency room for evaluation. This is the safest place for a person in danger, as doctors are immediately available and medication can be administered to control or avoid difficult behavior or injury.

4) If the family does not feel that an emergency response is needed, recommend that they call their family physician, who often has a medical history on the parishioner and a history of trust with the family. The family doctor may suggest the next step, possibly recommending a psychiatrist and referring the family. Psychiatrists are trained medical doctors who specialize in mental illness. They are the only people (other than regular physicians) who can prescribe medication and are trained in what kinds of medication work most effectively in a given emergency.

5) Psychologists and pastoral counselors are helpful for counseling the parishioner, but neither can prescribe medication. Their contribution is vital but of a different kind. They work as a team with psychiatrists and may be able to give more of their time to the patient.

6) If the family is afraid for the parishioner's safety or their own, offer to call paramedics to their home, and ask if you (or someone the parishioner knows well) may come and sit with the family until care arrives.

7) Refer to **Hospitalization and Emotional Illness** for details on visiting a mental hospital, interpreting the situation to the church office, and notifying the proper people with the family's permission.

8) Remember that mental illness is frightening to a family, so help them understand that the problem is not someone's fault or something to be ashamed of but a long-term care and recovery issue that deserves medical attention, support care for the individual and family, and time for healing.

9) Help the family gain insight and understanding into the nature of the disease or malady the person faces, and offer them prayer and support during the trauma of discovery of the illness, initial hospitalization, and long-term care.

10) Encourage the family to talk about their concerns and fears, and teach them to reach out to friends during this time. Families are often unaware of the emotional drain and spiritual energy required to manage mental disorder as a family.

For further reading:

Wayne E. Oates, *The Religious Care of the Psychiatric Patient* (Philadelphia: The Westminster Press, 1981).

Bob Phillips, *What To Do Until the Psychiatrist Comes* (Eugene OR: Harvest House Publishers, 1995).

Panic/Anxiety Attacks

1) You may receive an urgent call from a parishioner experiencing a panic attack or from a frightened family member witnessing the attack. Your calm and even voice will assure them of your help.

2) Panic attacks have no clear origin, and can disturb folks at any age, but tend to affect young adults, and young women three times as often as young men. Some of the physiological features are shortness of breath (hyperventilation), insomnia, faster heartbeat, lack of appetite, shaking, dizziness, numbness, chest pain, choking, sweating, fear of being alone, preoccupation and lack of capacity to focus, general anxious feeling, sense of being overwhelmed by too much to do in too little time, and restlessness.

3) People struggling with panic attacks need reassurance and presence. Make sure they are not alone, and ask if they have access to a doctor who can give them a general examination to rule out other problems. The doctor may give them a mild sedative prescription to reduce the general anxiety.

4) Victims of panic attacks not only need medication and friendship, they need some form of counseling, preferably short and frequent visits. Ask them if they have a pastor or pastoral counselor they trust, or refer them to a therapist.

5) Assure them that you remain available, but that they need continuous professional care and medication to get them past the sudden onsets of anxiety and panic. Keep in touch by calling them frequently for brief conversations.

6) Though we understand little about panic/anxiety attacks, they seem to be triggered by fears that exceed the patient's capacity to cope. People under pressure sometimes discover their limits with a "panic attack" signal, which acts as a flashing yellow light warning the person that they have arrived at the edge of their resources and need to get help.

7) Panic attack victims also practice the repetition of destructive thought patterns that accentuate the anxiety. "I won't be able to control myself." "I will pass out at any moment." "I'm going to be paralyzed by fear." "I'm going to go crazy." "I'm going to scream or act foolish." "I'm going to throw up and embarrass myself." These are some of the most common recurring disturbing thoughts.

8) Reassure panic attack victims that they can regain control and that they are not abnormal. Until they can gain equilibrium with medication and counseling, coach them to breathe slowly, to be aware of what they keep saying to themselves that scares them, and to ask themselves what they are truly afraid might happen to them. Facing a specific fear reduces its size and power.

9) All human beings sometimes reach their own limitations, and the caring God of the Bible instituted the Sabbath in order to help all creatures remember that they need rest and recovery. Remind anxious parishioners that Jesus Christ himself rested, taking time to be by himself after a busy day (Mark 6:31), pushing off in a boat so he could sleep (Matthew 8:23-24), and even leaving town so he could gain some moments of recovery (Mark 7:24).

10) Help victims of panic attacks not to expect recovery too quickly. They can find relief almost immediately, but they will need to employ

patience to conquer fears and anxieties over a period of time—one conquest at a time. Assist them in setting realistic goals about regaining control. "I will make it through this day until 6 P.M. without panicking." "I will allow myself to sleep tonight for at least five hours, and celebrate when I do !" "I will give myself about thirty minutes to move through this anxious feeling, and then I will settle down and gain some peace."

11) When the panic-stricken person calls you, out of breath and afraid, remind them to slow down, to breathe regularly, and to tell themselves that they will make it through the fear. After talking with them for a few minutes, ask if they are taking their medication. Some parishioners fear " getting hooked" on a medication, and they quit taking it too early. Most prescribed drugs for panic attacks would have to be taken in enormous dosages to become addictive.

12) Remember to care for the family and friends of the anxiety victim. They become anxious themselves and need suggestions about what to do to help. Also give them permission to take turns caring for the anxious parishioner to avoid overextending themselves or developing resentment and frustration toward the victim (see **Compassion Fatigue**).

13) Some family members (or friends) begin to suspect the afflicted person of "trying to get attention," or of consuming the family energy totally on themselves. Sometimes the family needs pastoral interpretation and care.

For further reading:
Susan Heitler, *Anxiety: Friend or Foe?* (Denver: Listen to Learn Audiotapes, Atrium Publishers Group, 1994) 1-800-919-8899.

Stanley Rachman, *Anxiety* (New York: Taylor & Francis, 1998).

Stanley Rachman & Padmal de Silva, *Panic Disorder: The Facts* (Vancouver, British Columbia: Oxford University Press, 1996).

Walton T. Roth, ed., *Treating Anxiety Disorders* (San Francisco: Jossey-Bass, 1996).

Rape

1) Victims of rape have their entire sense of security shattered, feel invaded and violated emotionally and physically, struggle with trust and safety, experience intense anger, guilt, and shame, and do not want to be alone.

2) One in three women in our society is raped (though men can be raped as well), and the incidence of sexual abuse, molestation, and rape is a serious problem in our communities (see Sexual Abuse).

3) Rape is a crime of violence, not simply sexual misconduct. Although rapists engage in what seems to be a sexual act with their abusive behavior, the primary intention is control, hostility, power, and violence.

4) Rape victims are often silent because they are either embarrassed, stunned, or fear not being taken seriously. Common myths about rape are:

• women can only be raped if they wish to be (either consciously or subconsciously);
• women who are raped "asked for it" by the particular way they acted or dressed;
• only people of lower social class or moral standards are raped.

5) The majority of rape victims are attacked by an acquaintance or friend and, more often than not, in their own home. They experience most of the symptoms of grief (see **Grief**), along with the normal

responses to an act of physical violence. Almost all victims are female, although male victims also struggle with the trauma, especially in seg- regated prison systems.

6) If you know that someone has been raped, one of the first acts of care you may extend is to check on their well-being and determine if they have had a physical examination by a doctor. A physician not only can discover if a victim needs to be treated for their injuries, but also can provide evidence that can be used against a rapist in a crimi- nal investigation.

7) Women who have been raped need the specific care of people who most understand their trauma, and female counselors and caregivers offer distinct advantages in the care of a survivor. Organizations such as Rape Crisis Centers and Citizens For Action Against Sexual Assault (CAASA) are among several groups who provide immediate care/counseling, appropriate medical referral, and group support for victims. Many survivors prefer to visit their own doctor if they have already established a relationship of trust.

8) Some survivors need anonymity and confidentiality first. They may prefer to visit a doctor whom they may not need to see again (offered through rape survival groups).

9) Exercise caution and keen awareness of your physical movement and touch with a survivor of rape. People who have been violated may not want to be hugged (though they need safe hugs!), and may find it difficult to accept any expression of affection—especially from a person of the opposite gender.

10) Because women are dazed and stressed by the violence of rape, they may wait to report it and to talk about it (even years). Encourage survivors to express their feelings, and acknowledge their right to feel anger, betrayal, helplessness, and a deep rage (see **Anger**).

11) Sometimes victims of rape struggle with how to tell their families about the violation. They may need the courage of your presence, words that identify the traumatic event, and a few comments that will help the family know how to respond to the survivor. You may need to assist a victim in determining how they will convey this difficult experience to their family.

12) If a rape survivor resists getting counseling care, gently insist that they care for themselves enough to choose some way of processing their pain—individual counseling with someone they already know and trust, counseling care with a trained rape counselor (check with Rape Crisis Centers or your United Way agency for a referral), pastoral counseling at a center, ongoing sessions with a minister (preferably of the same gender), or a group support program available through one of several community agencies (ask county service centers).

13) Counseling is important, even necessary, because victims of rape often have a delayed emotional and spiritual reaction to rape. They slowly begin to get in touch with their anger, bitterness, helplessness, fear, pain, and sense of loss over the brutalizing act. They frequently have nightmares, depression, anxiety bouts, and cycles of deep sadness. They need to process and expel the pain and agony they carry inside.

14) Help survivors by interpreting their trauma to family members and friends as you have permission to do so. Some family members transpose their helpless feelings of anger onto the victim, as if the person could have avoided the event. Some friends want the victim to "get over it" and move on, as if it were not the traumatizing experience of a lifetime.

For further reading:

Henry Cloud & John Townsend, *Safe People* (Grand Rapids MI: Zondervan, 1996).

Carrie Doehring, *Taking Care: Monitoring Power Dynamics & Relational Boundaries* (Nashville: Abingdon, 1995).

Gina O'Connell Higgins, *Resilient Adults: Overcoming a Cruel Past* (San Francisco: Jossey-Bass, 1995).

Harriet G. Lerner, *The Dance of Anger* (New York: Harper & Row, 1985).

Jeanne Stevenson Moessner, ed., *Through the Eyes of Women* (Minneapolis: Fortress Press, 1996).

Stress

1) When a parishioner calls for help because someone in the family is stressed, listen patiently and try to calm them. Stressed people usually feel overwhelmed, lose perspective, reach the end of their coping capacities, and struggle emotionally and physically to regain a balance in their lives.

2) Stress activates the body's "fight or flight" immune system; physical symptoms include hyperventilating, irritability, strained voice and tight muscles, preoccupation, difficulty with concentration and memory, sense of urgency, hyperactivity, low patience and tolerance, etc. Prominent causes of stress are listed below.

• The primary cause of stress is an internal (self) evaluation that a situation(s) exceeds one's capacity to cope with it. Rapid change can challenge people's equilibrium. We respond to change physiologically and emotionally; anxiety, depression, irritability, rapid mood swings, and anger tend to follow.
• We live in environments that can produce physical stressors such as noise, crowding, hunger, insomnia, and pollution.
• Work or organizational stressors include group demands, deadlines, expectations, excessive work hours, competition, and isolation.
• Some of our stresses are interpersonal: angry bosses or coworkers, critical and demanding people, aggressive or abusive cohorts, pessimistic people, troubled relationships, etc.
• We also create stress by placing unrealistic demands on ourselves (irrational guilt, inaccurate perceptions, put-downs, negative self-talk).

3) One of the first ways we can help stressed people is to ask them to focus on their most pressing problem. Some people stress over things that are not urgent. Ask, "What is your greatest concern (worry) right now?" They may mention four or five. Then ask, "If you could choose which one of those issues needs to be dealt with first, which would it be?"

4) By helping them choose which issue they must deal with first, you reduce their feeling that they face more than they can handle at the moment.

5) Also ask about the importance of the issues that cause stress. Are they really worth getting so upset and worried?

6) Next ask what they can do to help themselves work on the identified issue. Sometimes we stress about events over which we have no control and no power to change. Ask, "In what way is stressing or worrying about this issue helping your cause?"

7) Leslie Charles has identified "ten main stressors" in daily living (C. Leslie Charles, *Why Is Everyone So Cranky* [New York: Hyperian Press, 2001]):

• Compressed time due to hectic daily schedules
• Communication overload resulting from an overabundance of information
• Disconnection from significant relationships
• Cost and enticement: consumer pressure to accumulate/earn/spend
• Competition for adequacy/place/recognition
• Depersonalization due to rudeness, loss of respect
• Dependence on technology resulting from a pace of life that requires flawless performance, more output
• Change that happens at a quicker pace and is out of our control
• Trendiness: societal pressure to entertain/keep up/come of age
• Complexity due to balancing more demands than ever

8) Teach your parishioner about stress management. The body has restorative powers. Guide them to slow down, stop rushing through life, and do exercises for destressing through relaxation.

9) Ask the person to take a careful look at their schedule—what needs to be done first, what can be postponed, what urgency they may be creating, and whether they are overextended in their commitments.

10) Ask them about rest/sleep patterns and eating habits.

11) Remind them that one of the dimensions of faith is trusting yourself to the future one task and day at a time — "sufficient unto the day is the evil thereof" (Matthew 6:34 KJV).

Leslie Charles's Stress-Screening Questions
1. Feel continually rushed and pressed for time?
2. Been awhile since you did anything fun?
3. Become more irritable or impatient over the last couple of years?
4. Neglecting your health in any way?
5. Feel dissatisfied or discontent with the past year?
6. Feel apprehensive about this year?
7. A pending change in your life you've been resisting or avoiding?
8. A relationship in your life that needs attention?
9. Working more and enjoying it less?
10. Plagued with the nagging sensation that something is missing in your life?
11. Headaches/anxiety/muscular tension/sleep/stomach/spending/appetite/irritability/tight, clenched jaw/worries/distracted/resentful?

How to Relax
1. Live with purpose. Have a sense of who you are and what you live for.
2. Enhance self-awareness.
3. Quit judging others. Take energy to work on you.
4. Capitalize on your own wisdom.

5. Make conscious choices and avoid seeing yourself as a victim.

6. Think of yourself as skilled and adequate in many things—you are.

7. Surround yourself with support; choose safe people and avoid naysayers.

8. Replace negative emotions with positive ones. Quit trivial worrying.

9. Stay connected. Invest in relationships; don't isolate yourself.

10. Choose compassion. Contempt and kindness are hard to hold together.

11. Ask yourself: Is this a small, medium, or a large annoyance?

12. Ask yourself: How upset do I want to get, and for how long?

For further reading:

David Elkind, *Ties That Stress* (New Haven CT: Harvard University Press, 1994).

Mary Dell Miles, *Stress* (Nashville: Abingdon Press, 1994).

Suicide

Suicide Attempt

1) One of the greatest challenges in caregiving is facing the attempted (or successful) suicide of a parishioner or their family member. A person may call and express concern about a loved one whom they fear is considering suicide. Remember the following most common indicators of a suicidal person.

- Repeats comments about suicide, wishing they were dead, or wondering if their family would be better off without them
- Depression; physical and emotional withdrawal
- Dramatic change in sleeping and eating habits; giving away items or valuables dear to them
- Abuse of medication
- Tendency toward recurring tears, deep sadness, and discouragement
- Repeated comments or struggle with a sense of hopelessness
- Evidence that the individual is in a great deal of pain (emotional)
- History of previously attempted suicide
- Overwhelming stress
- Isolation and detachment from a community of care
- Member of an unstable (dysfunctional) family
- Rewriting a will; planning their own funeral

2) Following an assessment of these indicators, consider any initiative from a suicidal person as an act of trust. Remain calm, listen intently, and ask them direct questions. It is normal for you to feel somewhat

anxious when you first hear their comments. Try to avoid overanxious responses, which increase the discomfort of the parishioner.

3) Don't try to solve the suicidal person's problems. Your goal is to get them to professional help. Connect emotionally with the person, and empathize with their pain. "You must be in a great deal of pain. Can you tell me what's causing you such distress?"

4) When the parishioner talks about feelings of hopelessness and discouragement, identify their solution (taking their own life) as only one of many options. Help them think about other choices for a moment. Most suicidals think there is only one "solution" to their situation.

5) Invite the struggling friend to reflect on their worries and help them to examine them more clearly if possible. "Martha, you've mentioned a number of heavy concerns, and your pain seems enormous. How are you managing all of this, and which one is bothering you the most?"

6) Don't be afraid to ask a depressed (suicidal) person if they have thought of suicide or "harming" themselves. "Have you had any thoughts about hurting yourself, Jim?" It will not give them any new ideas, and it will tell you whether they are seriously at risk and need intervention such as immediate care or hospitalization. Suicidal people are relieved that the subject can be mentioned and that they can express some of their fears. Remember, you don't need to solve this issue for them. You are there to protect them from hurting themselves.

7) When a deeply depressed person needs immediate help to control self-destructive behavior, review their choices with them. "It sounds like you need some care to help you get through all this pain. One option is for us to get you to a hospital, where you can get some medication and sleep better. Then you can look at your problems and choices in the morning. Or, we can get you to a doctor who will take a few minutes and decide if you can still stay at home—with some medication, and with family or friends nearby—until you can get to a

counselor and explore some of your worries. Or do you think you're going to be able to manage all this some other way?"

8) A person dealing with three or four of the indicators mentioned on page 131 should not be left alone. They should only be given a choice to quit talking with you (or leave) if they have someone with them and if they promise to call you, a family member, or 911 if they begin to lose control of destructive thoughts and behaviors and attempt to harm themselves.

9) If a depressed parishioner refuses to cooperate with being hospitalized and no family member is available, volunteer to go with them to the hospital. Call 911 for assistance in getting them there under proper supervision. Do not attempt to drive a suicidal friend to a hospital by yourself, unless you have no other option available. In such a case, use a cell phone or other phone to tell a pastor, deacon, or elder about the problem and that you are taking the person to get help. Ask them to have someone meet you both at the medical facility.

10) Remember that a family member has to sign a reluctant parishioner into an institution in order to detain the person against their will. Only police officers and a doctor have the same authority.

11) Read **Hospitalization and Emotional Illness** for advice on when and how to visit a hospitalized parishioner.

For further reading:
G. Lloyd & Gwendolyn C. Carr, *The Fierce Goodbye* (Downer's Grove IL: InterVarsity Press, 1990).

John H. Hewett, *After Suicide* (Philadelphia: Westminster Press, 1980).

Charles M. Sheldon, *Pastoral Counseling with Adolescents & Young Adults* (New Yorlc: Crossroad, 1995).

Howard Rosenthal, *Not With My Life I Don't: Preventing Your Suicide and That of Others* (Muncie IN: Accelerated Development Inc., 1988).

After Suicide Occurs

1) When a suicide has already occurred, the surviving family and close friends face not only the trauma of sudden loss (see **Grief**), but the complications of guilt, shame, and several unacknowledged issues.

2) A suicide survivor is anyone who grieves the loss of someone who took their own life. More people kill themselves (suicide) in this country than are killed by someone else (homicide).

3) The survivor must confront a gaping hole that cannot be replaced by anyone else, and an overwhelming sense of pain, anxiety, and heartache. Survivors need continued care. They will grieve for a long time, and many of their friends will say nothing to them for fear of saying the wrong thing. Help friends share a word of care. "I don't know what to say, but I continue to think about you and pray for you."

4) Help survivors understand that there are few people who can understand how they feel. Help them know that grief will take a long time and that depression is a normal, if painful, reaction to such a traumatic and seemingly senseless event.

5) Bewilderment and guilt are natural reactions among family members and friends, who try somehow to understand why the person committed suicide, or if they themselves could have been more responsible and prevented the death. We cannot keep someone from committing suicide if they want to, but loved ones struggle to deal with the complicated mystery of such a disturbing way to die.

6) Nightmares, bouts with guilt, and deep feelings of sadness occur repeatedly. If the deceased person suffered with emotional pain for a long time, the survivor may feel relieved that the person is not hurting anymore. Then they feel guilty for feeling relieved.

7) Anniversaries and holidays can be quite difficult for the survivors; those left behind not only remember a birthday or a special occasion, but the day of the death on a weekly, then monthly, then annual basis. A note or a phone call can mean a great deal, especially with a prayer and a wish for God's presence to comfort them.

8) Let a minister help survivors learn how to talk with children and young people about suicide. Though some people prefer to pretend that a death was not suicide, it takes a great deal of energy to hide that reality. Telling the truth without long explanations benefits family and friends.

9) One of the best gifts surviving adults can offer young people and children in their communities (churches) is to model the normal expressions of grief: sadness, tears, numbness, depression, anger, guilt, helplessness, painful memories, privacy, and processing with words. Children and youth not only learn from such adult behaviors about what is normal in grief, but are reassured that their own similar thoughts and feelings are natural and appropriate (and can be shared!).

10) Family members and friends at some point will inquire or wonder about God and suicide. A prevailing opinion about suicide is that it is an unforgivable sin. Make sure a pastor (or a mature layperson) is available to spend time interpreting the love and grace of God in the face of suicide. After all, how can any of us know what takes place between God and a dying person in the agony of a pain sufficient enough to elicit suicide? Contrary to what some people may think, the Bible says little about suicide, treating is mostly as an occurrence in the struggle with human failure (1 Samuel 31:4; 1 Kings 19:4; Matthew 27:3-5).

11) An organization called Suicide Awareness/Voices of Education (SAVE), available in some localities, offers support groups for survivors of suicide. Your town may have an American Suicide Foundation support group or one established by the American Association of Suicidology. If a support group is not available for

survivor recovery, ask clergy and congregations in your area to help provide one, and invite suicide survivors to join grief support groups similar to it.

For further reading:

Ann Marie Putter, ed., *The Memorial Rituals Book For Healing and Hope* (New York: Baywood Publishing Co., 2000).

Adina Wrobleski, *Suicide: Survivors (A Guide for Those Left Behind)* (Minneapolis: Afterwords Publishing, 1991).

Howard Stone, *Suicide & Grief* (Philadelphia: Fortress Press, 1972).

Appendix:
Principles in Counseling

1) Be alert to ministry invitations. People "ask" us into their lives in disguised ways, with quiet requests and fearful misgivings.

2) Be willing to become involved, but also to keep your distance. Whose needs are being met—yours or theirs?

3) The presenting problem is not necessarily the most critical problem. Listen and wait for more. Then ask, "Is this what you are most concerned about?"

4) Flexibility and open-mindedness are essential. Our business is to open doors, not close them.

5) Nonjudgmental attitudes facilitate disclosure and make options more visible. Lowering the parishioner's anxiety helps them see their options and choose more effectively.

6) A marriage may be helped if only one partner is willing to work; a family may be helped if only one person in it is willing to grow; a child or youth may be helped even if a family will not cooperate.

7) The behavior problems of a child or youth may often reflect the dysfunctional struggle of the family.

8) At first, do more listening and less talking—ask, identify, clarify, summarize.

9) Avoid becoming too supportive too quickly; don't do for people what they can do for themselves.

10) Seek to recognize your own anxieties and fears.

11) Treat every person as a unique individual. Become a student of their situation.

12) Avoid prescribing "treatment" without adequate evaluation. The problem may not be what you first think it is.

13) Aid the person in planning a strategy or solution, but don't do it for them. Assist those with multiple problems to choose the issue they most need to resolve first.

14) If you are providing regular support or counseling, continue as long as necessary, but release the person to their own strength as soon as you are not needed in that role.

15) Make appropriate referrals; don't help beyond your capacity (doctors don't either); balance trust with compassion and challenge.

16) Avoid the notion that you are totally responsible for how well things turn out.

17) Be willing to be wrong.

18) Remain attentive and calm when tested. Remind yourself that you did not create anyone's feelings, and ask yourself what energy or pain drives what they say and do.

19) Be aware of your own limitations and alert to your signs of vulnerability.

20) Express appropriate ongoing care, but allow people privacy and distance as needed.

21) Act as a representative of God; people often already have friends but no pastors.

Stress/Change Scale

This "impact of stress" scale was developed by Thomas H. Holmes, M.D., and modified several times. The study was undertaken to assess the stress impact that different events have on individuals, with an assumption that several issues might occur at the same time. Holmes suggested that an accumulated scale of 300 points or more would stress a person to the point of incapacity to function adequately.

Death of a child 100
Death of a spouse...92
Divorce 73
Marital separation 65
Jail term 63
Death of a close family member 63
Personal injury or illness..................................53
Marriage...50
Loss of job (termination) 49
Marital reconciliation 45
Retirement 45
Pregnancy...45
Geographical move...42
Sexual adjustments 39
Gain of a new family member 39
Business readjustment 39
Change in financial status.................................38
Death of a close friend 37
Change to different line of work.......................36
Change in number of arguments with spouse....35
Mortgage over $40,000 dollars.........................31
Foreclosure of loan or bankruptcy 30
Son or daughter leaving home 29
Trouble with in-laws...29

The main stressors are finances, fatigue, grief, abandonment, isolation, self-doubt, depression, and disengagement.

Levels of Care

1) Sometimes caregivers become anxious about the level of care they can provide. They may feel inadequate to attend to a variety of difficult needs parishioners face.

2) Because church members often trust deacons and other lay leaders more than these leaders trust themselves, and because different levels of care require less "taught" skills and more compassionate listening, here are some guidelines for different levels in which you may be invited to participate. Evaluate these levels in light of your own abilities; choose at what level you can best offer help and at what level you need to seek additional help for the person. All levels are an adaptation of Wayne Oates' suggestions, mentioned on the following pages.

- *Level of friendship:* Many important acts of care begin in informal conversations that start in the grocery store aisle, the soccer field, the church outing, or the church parking lot. This level of care is called friendship because it begins in the informal conversations of everyday living (an invitation to lunch, a pause for a cup of coffee). These conversations are the foundation for trust, interest, and common ground that lay the groundwork for times when deeper care is needed.

• *Level of comfort:* When tragedy and change jar people's routines, parishioners look for comfort and reassurance from those they feel closest to or trust the most. During death, loss, and traumatic events, we are suddenly or quietly invited into the "inner sanctum" of a person's life at moments when they feel most fragile and need support. Words of support, active listening, and a quiet, peaceful presence benefit these people the most.

• *Level of confession:* Burdened by the weight of a troubling issue, parishioners sometimes move from casual conversations to issues of deep significance for them. Expressing trust and vulnerability as they share important experiences, people who choose to tell us the deeper thoughts and struggles of their lives at this level are engaging us in a "priestly" function. They want us to listen to their struggles, hear their confrontation with a failure or wrong, and—if we are clergy—assure them of forgiveness and pardon for their fault. Sometimes a trusting parishioner tells a caregiver more than they want to know. If this occurs, the caregiver must appropriately suggest to the person that they talk confidentially with a professional about their struggle.

• *Level of teaching:* Parishioners sometimes struggle with issues because they are uninformed or don't have access to helpful information; they need us as a bridge to connect them with helpful resources. If they need help understanding Scripture, we can guide them to ministers and pastoral counselors trained to assist in such issues; if the questions are medical, we can encourage them to seek insight from medical experts; if they struggle with emotional and spiritual issues, we can guide them to spiritual advisors. Sometimes people need community support and resources that we can suggest to them. At this level of care, we are often "ministers of introduction," as Wayne Oates described us (*The Christian Pastor* [Philadelphia: Westminster Press, 1983]).

• *Level of brief support dialogue:* Some people need our attention as they wrestle with a particular issue, and we need to provide them with a quiet place where they may speak and we may hear their need. Clergy are often invited into these more structured conversations at the back of the sanctuary after a worship service. This level of dialogue is more involved, for it requires a capacity and skill in making a parishioner feel accepted, listening carefully while an issue is identified and explained, helping the person explore what options are available in dealing with the issue, and giving some conclusion to the conversation that commits the parishioner and the caregiver to responsibilities they assume.

• *Level of counseling:* This deeper level of care can only be provided by professional counselors and therapists trained to delve into a problem for an extended period of tirne (several counseling sessions) in a formal arrangement where appointments are made, specific goals are set, and a structured therapeutic plan is agreed upon. Caregivers can often use the "brief support dialogue" as a way to determine if extensive counseling care is needed and a way to discover what kind of counseling the parishioner needs.

For further reading:
Wayne E. Oates, *The Christian Pastor* (Philadelphia: Westminster Press, 1983).

Listening and Talking Skills

Specific Ways to Improve Listening (adapted from Miller, Miller, Nunnally, & Wackman, *Talking & Listening Together*):

1) Actions: Practice sustained eye contact with the person with whom we are in conversation (but don't stare!). Convey a calm and relaxed posture; be attentive, acknowledging their responses and inviting comments/questions; summarize what they tell you to be sure you understand; be respectful, truthful, open, clear, tactful, and understanding.

2) Listening skills:

- pay attention to the person (look, listen, track feeling and communi cation of their gestures);
- acknowledge what they say (use head or gesture movements, words) and be aware of feelings you detect behind the words;
- invite more information and sharing by facial expression, inquiry, show of interest;
- summarize what they said, both for accuracy and to communicate your awareness;
- ask open-ended questions, which evoke more than simple "yes" and "no" responses and encourage the person to share more ("What did you like most about the seminar?" instead of "Did you like the seminar?").

3) Four basic purposes of conversation:

Purpose 1: Small talk. Maintenance of distance and comfort-seeking. Our primary goal is to be pleasant but uninvolved emotionally. Such talk is necessary for "breaking the ice," but safe and superficial. Examples: hello/goodbye, passing time, storytelling, joking, catching up, sharing events of the day, discussing biographical data, personal traits, habits, appearances, weather, etc.

Purpose 2: Control/Change talk. Designed mainly to direct, instruct, or guide someone to do what we want. We usually want to control the conversation or the person and set the limits ourselves. This is useful for directing someone, but not for listening to someone or learning what they are thinking. Examples: directing, setting expectations, establishing boundaries, advising, prescribing, cautioning, warning, advocating, selling, assuming, speaking for others, praising.

Purpose 3: Search/explore talk. Concerned with gathering perceptions, learning different opinions, exploring points of view, sizing up options, seeking to understand. Excellent for initial caregiving. Involves asking questions, inviting person to say more. Examples:

identifying issues, analyzing causes, giving impressions, requesting interpretations, generating possibilities, evaluating options, clarifying, exploring possibilities.

Purpose 4: Involved/committed talk. Willing to take risks in becoming more invested in the conversation and the relationship. We pay attention to emotional content in the dialogue, share our feelings and listen attentively to theirs, make clear commitments, and take responsibility for our thoughts and feelings, our intentions and behaviors, asking them to do the same. Examples: focusing on issue, identifying tension, acknowledging differences, requesting feedback, giving feedback, expressing appreciation, sharing vulnerability, asking for change, taking responsibility for our own contribution/response, apologizing/asking forgiveness, giving support, making decisions.

Become more aware of the particular purpose you have in mind when you start a conversation, and choose more consciously which purpose (style) will accomplish what you want to do in your caregiving conversation. All four purposes are useful and have their place. Communication experts tell us that we usually spend most of our time in purposes 1 and 2. If we are to help others effectively, we must move further than small and manipulative talk in our conversations.

4) Five Ways to Listen Attentively:

Sensations: Sight, sound, smell, taste, and touch. Observing what we see, how people look, what we hear, how they act, how they make contact.

Thoughts: We listen to the thoughts people express in order to understand them better. The thoughts people share convey their beliefs, interpretations, and expectations.
Feelings: Spontaneous responses to sensations, thoughts, or wants in a situation. They provide information about us and are often based on our thoughts, interpretations, and perceptions.

Wants/Wishes: Our desires and wishes for ourselves and others and for relationships. Hopes, goals, motives, intentions. Usually "to be," "to do," and "to have."

Actions: Our behavior, saying or doing, and what it "says" about us.

For further reading:
Miller, et al., *Talking & Listening Together* (Littleton CO: Interpersonal Communications Programs, 1991).

John Savage, *Listening & Caring Skills in Ministry* (Nashville: Abingdon, 1996).

Conflict Resolution

1) When a family or individuals experience conflict and ask you for help, be aware that most people fear conflict and try to avoid it. Reasons for avoiding conflict:

• Most of our experiences with conflict have produced pain.
• People who choose to face conflict often feel that they lose power.
• Many people who encounter conflict endure broken or damaged relationships due to the ways they tried to resolve conflict.
• Some attempts at resolving differences have caused tension and appear hopeless.
• Working on conflict takes energy and time and is unpleasant.

2) Remind parishioners that conflict actually reflects our diversity; we were made in the image of God. Conflict can be positive (redemptive) when it is used to clarify a relationship, to provide additional ways of thinking and options for actions that need consideration, and to affirm the importance of an issue or point of view a person holds.

3) As a declaration of a different point of view, conflict is a way of stating that we think for ourselves and that we are a separate self with an individual contribution to make.

4) Five common ineffective ways to resolve conflict:

- The conquest approach: labels opposite sides "winners" and "losers"
- The avoidance approach: postpones the issue and ignores differences
- The argumentative approach: offers demands and concessions
- The "quick-fixer" approach: is driven by anxiety and simplifies the differences
- The role-keeper approach: uses power to control the outcome and reduces the opportunity for dialogue

5) Help people in conflict understand that there are several issues at work when we examine our differences:

- People are not alike; we have varied backgrounds.
- Needs and desires shape a person's point of view.
- Perceptions of a situation vary depending on circumstances.
- Goals or purposes in a conversation may be quite different from person to person.
- Values and principles affect how two points of view emerge.
- Feelings and emotions color differences of opinion.
- Personal stress and other internal struggles affect reactions.

6) Offer these steps for those who struggle with conflict and look for constructive ways to resolve their differences:

- Create an effective atmosphere by suggesting a good setting and time for dialogue.
- Clarify the perceptions of those involved. Ask the people what their goals and perceptions are, acknowledge their thoughts and feelings, and listen to each other's point of view.
- Identify the needs and feelings both individuals have in the conflict.
- Share power and authority in the conversation, and give each other the respect of listening to both points of view.
- Avoid gestures and a tone of voice that suggests "attacking," and try to perceive the opposing person as not attacking you.
- Try to remain focused on an issue and not attack a person.

- If feeling tense, try to use humor on yourself (not the other person).
- Volunteer to take some responsibility for the differences, and share your commitment as a Christian to do your part to allow your neighbor a different opinion.
- If possible, make covenants to each other that hold mutual benefits ("I'll try not to sound like this is the only way to do it"/and "I'll try to understand your point of view, even though I strongly disagree with you on this").

7) Help your parishioners by identifying frequent problems in conflict that make resolution more difficult:

- displays of anger, losing control over intensity of words, behavior
- denying that there is a conflict, making it impossible to examine
- rejection of the other person, which increases distance
- unwillingness to cooperate with efforts for dialogue (Matthew 18:15-18, Galatians 6:1-5)
- abusive or vindictive attitudes toward another, which creates an atmosphere of suspicion and tension
- grief experience that affects initiative and responses
- attitude of superiority or self-righteousness that eliminates mutual respect

8) An intense and long-held conflict drains its participants of energy and focus and requires professional help to overcome. Offer your services as a mediator only to begin conversations of reconciliation. Remember that you are not responsible for the resolution of the conflict; the people involved in the conflict are responsible.

For further reading:
Daniel G. Bagby, *Understanding Anger in the Church* (Nashville: Broadman, 1979).
Roberta Gilbert, *Extraordinary Relationships* (New York: John Wiley & Sons, 1992).
Dudley Weeks, *Conflict Resolution* (New York: Penguin/Putnam, 1992).

Using the Bible and Prayer in Pastoral Care

The Bible

1) Remember that the Scriptures hold powerful symbolic and faith values for many people. Your use of them can bring great comfort and strength to people in crises. Secure permission when you plan to read, and avoid reading for long periods of time, especially if the person is heavily medicated.

2) In pastoral visitation, a pocket-sized copy of the Bible (perhaps New Testament & Psalms) may be useful as a means of identifying your role visually to a confused, disoriented, or hearing impaired person. It should not be used as a means of avoiding personal contact or as a "magical" book. Asking for the parishioner's Bible may help you note what passages they have marked as valuable to them.

3) A careful study of people and events in the Bible will help a caregiver refer to appropriate biblical truths without having to quote a specific passage. For example, both the obvious (Job), and the less obvious (Paul) can be helpful to someone struggling with pain. Spend time recording the different struggles of people in the Bible; your notes will be a useful "pastoral dictionary."

4) Remember that biblical passages parishioners mention may be useful as diagnostic information. What they say and what they remember or ask may reflect their struggles more accurately than anything else.

5) When reading Scripture in visits (or at funerals), ask what passages mean the most to a listener; it may also say something about them. When you read, read slowly and clearly, and remember to position yourself where they can hear. Avoid long passages of Scripture; listeners may lose interest or become overburdened and forget the passage more easily.

6) Make sure you are reading to help your parishioner, not to meet your own needs or avoid personal contact. The stories and words of the Bible can comfort those who have become bitter, angry, and afraid. It can soothe those who hurt, doubt, struggle, and give up. Scripture can strengthen people and give them faith in the midst of trial. It can remind believers that people in the Bible also struggled and hurt.

7) There may be a few passages of Scripture that mean enough to you (and others) that you might commit them to memory. Focus on shepherding needs if you choose to memorize verses—healing, guiding, reconciling, sustaining (four suggestions from Seward Hiltner, former professor at Princeton Seminary, in William R. Clebsch and Charles R. Jaekle's *Pastoral Care in Historical Perspective* [Englewood Cliffs NJ: Prentice Hall, 1964] 4-7).

8) Remember that there are people with a magical view of Scripture who sometimes use religious language when they are emotionally unstable. Not all religious conversation is "rational religion"; it may be a sign of mental illness.

For further reading:
Wayne E. Oates, *The Bible in Pastoral Care* (Philadelphia: Westminster, 1953); idem, *Where to Go for Help* (Philadelphia: Westminster, 1957).
Leslie Brandt, *Psalms Now* (St. Louis: Concordia Press, 1996).

Prayer
1) Occasionally, a prayer early in a conversation not only reassures a parishioner that you truly represent the church, but also allows you to discover their major concerns. You might ask, "I can see that you are distressed. Can I pray for something in particular?" Listen to their answer. Take it seriously.
2) Sometimes we can use Paul's example of telling people that we are going to pray for them and what we are going to pray about. Some example statements follow. Remember to be brief. "I'm going to be praying for you, that God may give you peace of mind during this

pressured time, and that you may sense God's presence when you feel most alone or isolated." "I will pray that God may give you courage and strength as you face some of the news you're waiting for, and that God will give your family sensitivity and understanding to help you in ways you most need help right now." "My prayer is that God will give you patience when you need it, wisdom for choices you may have, and comfort when you hurt and need relief." Sometimes the setting or situation is not conducive for praying at that moment, but you can state what you will be praying about. Such specific prayers also tell your friend that you have truly been listening to them.

3) Prayer can sometimes instruct and offer care to people with unmentioned needs that you surmise are there but that they have not acknowledged. Your prayer then helps them accept normal feelings they might try to deny; it may also assist them to understand how to pray for themselves. "Dear Lord, you understand this person's struggle as no one else does. Help her in this distress to trust you with her pain. When she is in pain, strengthen her through her anger and misery. When she wonders if you care, help her remember your agony as you watched your own son die and waited helplessly by. Remind her if she becomes impatient and frustrated with you that you love her enough to outlast all the bitterness she may feel, even as you did so many times with your beloved Israel…," etc.

4) Don't pray too long. Remember to pray for family members and expressed concerns. Avoid generalities.

5) Don't promise things in prayer you can't deliver and things that God may not deliver. When asked if you would pray that your patient may be delivered from terminal cancer (think about your own theology), respond: "I'll be glad to pray for your healing, and I know that miracles can happen. I will also pray that if it is not possible for you to heal, that God may grant you every possible comfort and the strength to face the pain you feel, and that God will walk with you as a sure presence even if it must be through the valley of the shadow of death."

For further reading:
Richard C. Cabot and Russell L. Dicks, *The Art of Ministering to the Sick* (New York: The MacMillan Co., 1944).

Michael Quoist, *New Prayers* (New York: Crossroad, 1995).

Compassion Fatigue

1) People who study caregivers have found that under the stress of caring for others, we tend to regress into one of three unhealthy habits:

- We begin to feel sorry for ourselves and resent the person for whom we are caring. We also resent others who are not carrying their part of the workload.
- We become depressed from exhaustion, lose perspective, and look to others to take over our job.
- We intensify our efforts, work harder, become almost compulsive about our work, and grow increasingly angry about the inability to conquer our fatigue.

2) Signs of compassion fatigue include irritability, resentment, anger disproportionate to events, frustration, daytime drowsiness, restlessness, preoccupation, depression, sudden outbursts, sarcasm, forgetfulness, isolation from people, and numbness. Centuries ago monks performing routine functions for years while experiencing isolation from human contact developed what their superiors called "acedia": a numbing detachment that rendered them spiritually dysfunctional.

3) What wears us out?

- *Exhaustion/Overextension:* Our hands grow tired from the constancy of our work. Like Moses, we don't know how to quit or where to go for help (Numbers 11:10-15).

- *Emotional Pain:* Our body system absorbs so much pain from caring for the wounded that we are saturated (Jesus experienced this; Mark 6:31).

- *Personal Grief:* Significant losses in our own lives require first energy, and strength is sapped before we have time to think of those for whom we care (2 Samuel 18:19-34).

- *Personal Stress:* Changes and transitions in our own lives extend beyond our capacity to manage anxiety (Job 6:1-13).

- *Moral Pain:* The unjust systems and relationships in our community or society assault our peace and destroy our hope for change (Luke 9:41).

- *Self-Doubt:* One event or an accumulation of events seduce us into believing that none of our efforts are of value (1 Kings 19:8-11).

- *Spiritual Drought:* Our faith resources appear irrelevant or void of meaning (Exodus 3:11-13).

- *Rejection Paralysis:* We become preoccupied with how people respond to our efforts of trying to help them, and eventually we're controlled by their responses to us (Matthew 23:37-39).

- *Excessive Identification:* Our passion over the sorrow and pain of others renders us dysfunctional (Mark 8:2-10).

- *Expectation Obsession:* We demand too much of ourselves. Must we help everyone and start or finish every service of care? (1 Corinthians 3:6-8)

4) Tired caregivers need to be reminded of God's purpose in the Sabbath, which was to rest people, rest the land, and gain perspective on creation, God, and daily living. People who constantly care for

others often fail to realize how much energy and time caregiving requires.

5) Help fatigued caregivers identify two important challenges: guilt and relief. People who care constantly for loved ones experience significant bouts of guilt whenever they consider "taking a break." We need to help faithful caregivers by reminding them that even Jesus, the older brother in the family, took time away from family cares to enjoy much-needed rest and relief.

6) Churches can help worn caregivers by providing coverage for them so that they can interrupt their daily care routines to gain relief, rest, and renewal. One or two hours of care provided by a Sunday school class or a friend can do much to alleviate temporary fatigue. Deacons and ministers can also assist families to involve other family members who may not be aware of the time and energy one person spends in the care of a needy loved one.

7) Families need help with the delicate issue of assessing when their personal resources are inadequate to continue care for someone, especially in their own home. Support groups for people who care for special children, confined adults, or chronically ill individuals are a blessing every community could organize. Help your congregation (or groups of congregations) create such a ministry.

8) Teach people the importance of rest for the sake of adequate caregiving. Like our muscles, which cramp when continually flexed and soon cease to function, our spirits deteriorate under constant pressure. Caregivers need time away from a strenuous task in order to provide more effective care for their loved ones.

9) If a caregiver in your community shows signs of compassion fatigue, help them understand that such experiences are normal,and help them find ways to gain recurring relief from constant "giving."

10) As a caregiver, you may sense that you are growing tired of hearing people's concerns and sorrows and becoming impatient or frustrated with people who turn to you for help. Take time to evaluate how tired you are, whether you are overextended, and how long it has been since you took a vacation, had a break, or distracted yourself from the burden of caring. You can rest and rejuvenate yourself by exercising, engaging in activities that entertain you, doing a few things regularly that give you pleasure, and renewing your soul.

For further reading:

Henry Cloud & John Townsend, *Boundaries* (Grand Rapids MI: Zondervan, 1992).

Vivian E. Greenberg, *Respecting Your Limits When Caring for Aging Parents* (San Francisco: Jossey-Bass, 1989).

Thomas Moore, *Care of the Soul* (New York: HarperCollins, 1992).

Conrad W. Weiser, *Healers Harmed & Harmful* (Minneapolis: Fortress, 1994).